Baking Solutions

Helpful Hints For Home Baking

By: Lyndal Power & Kenneth Power

YCART PUBLISHING, Oklahoma City, Oklahoma

Baking Solutions

HELPFUL HINTS FOR HOME BAKING

By Lyndal Power & Kenneth Power

Published by:

YCART PUBLISHING
P.O. Box 74980
Oklahoma City, Oklahoma 73147

First printing 1993

Printed in the United States of America.
Library of Congress Catalog Card Number: 92 - 64417
Power, Lyndal & Power, Kenneth
Baking Solutions: Helpful Hints For Home Baking
Lyndal Power & Kenneth Power — First ed.
Includes index
ISBN 1-880650-12-6

Contents

ABOUT THE AUTHORS

Kenneth and Lyndal are published short story fiction writers and have written hundreds of personalized articles for individual businesses in the course of their bakery consulting work. In 1991, Kenneth wrote **POWER BAKING**, *A Contemporary American Baking Manual,* for professional bakers. He considers, **BAKING SOLUTIONS**, to be the crown jewel of his and Lyndal's writing accomplishments.

Lyndal Power is a native Texan. She wears the hats of creative designer, computer artist, writer, baking consultant, editor, photographer, home maker and does all the necessary work that makes writing a book possible. Her baking skills keep Kenneth, their friends and families in a constant battle with their waist lines.

Lyndal's strong point is her people skills. She makes friends quickly and those friends provide the generous information, without which, this book would not exist.

Baking, writing and making new friends are Lyndal and Kenneth's passions, but they still find time to wrestle with their two Siberian Huskies, Natasha and Sue-Ki.

Solutions for good Baking

Have you ever wished you were blessed with "a born knack for baking?" Well, you can stop wishing—there is no such thing.

Skills in baking are learned—not born in a person. It takes no special gift or magic touch to become a good baker. It just takes learning and following a set of rules for each thing you bake.

Sure, some home bakers seemingly throw things together and achieve glorious results. But their secret is long practice and probably a lot of luck. Baking a particular item over and over again enables one to learn the look and feel of that item. This judgement takes the place of following step-by-step rules. However, when you give that person a new item to bake they must follow the rules or else face disaster.

Here, in this book, there are tested methods, tips, hints and answers to perfect baking. Whether you're a beginner or an expert, the things you learn here will make your baking better, easier and more fun.

It is love of the right method, the desire to do things with a reason—*in proven ways*, that has simplified home baking and its results more certain.

This book also teaches the step method involved in mixing many baked items from scratch or from a boxed pre-mix. If you will master using the correct steps—you will become an expert baker in no time at all.

"The most important thing to always remember

is that your baking environment is different from anyone else's. Your oven will bake differently, your mixer will mix differently, the temperature of the pre-mix ingredients or your fresh ingredients will be different. Even the humidity of your kitchen will be different. You are unique and because of this, the problems you face will be different from anyone else's."

Let's start with the basic rules and follow each one carefully.

1. Be orderly

Do your planning before you start. Choose your recipe, read it through carefully, understand it fully. Gather all the ingredients it calls for in their order. Assemble all the tools you will need for the job. Have a do-it-right attitude from the beginning and baking will become a joy instead of a job. The do-it-right attitude will take the worry out of baking.

2. Use the proper tools

The proper tools for the job will simplify baking. They enable you to do things more easily, more accurately. They speed up mixing and help you to achieve uniformly successful results.

3. Choose high quality ingredients

You can't do first rate work with second rate ingredients. What you put in is what you get. Make sure that your ingredients are fresh and are always of the highest quality.

4. Measure accurately

Correct measuring is a baking **MUST**. The best

ingredients in the world, the highest skill and the best tools cannot overcome poor measuring. If the recipe tells you to sift your flour—do it. If you don't, the flour will be of the wrong measure and your baked item will suffer. Measure spoons level unless told otherwise. Make sure that different sets of cups and spoons you will be using to make a recipe actually hold the same amounts. Some cups will differ by 1/8 a cup. This is more than enough to make a difference in your baking.

5. Mix carefully

There are several basic methods of mixing each baked item. Follow the recipe's directions to the letter and refer to this book for more information. Remember—everything you do in baking is done for a reason.

6. Know your pans, ovens, mixer, proper cooling and handling of each baked item you make.

The actual baking process is important. Proper pans, using them correctly, the right oven temperature, time for baking, correct cooling—all are vital to baking it right.

These are the rules you must know to bake with a reason— using proven ways. They are usually written into each recipe and must be followed to the letter.

BAKING'S GOLDEN RULE: *Your Baking Environment Is Always Different From Anyone Else's. The Things You Bake Will Always Be Unique To Your Environment.*

BAKING SOLUTIONS

BAKING SOLUTIONS is a problem solving reference book written by a *Master Professional Baker* and *Master Home Baker* for the home baker as well as advanced bakers.

A large percentage of baking today comes out of a box, can or sack, and ready-to-bake, but still — technique in baking is everything. The recipe's ingredients, whether in the form of a pre-mix, frozen or scratch, must follow specific methods of preparation, baking, and finishing.

BAKING SOLUTIONS is full of unique and informative comments on individual baked items. This makes problems associated with assembling the ingredients and following methods a thing of the past.

Each chapter of **BAKING SOLUTIONS** covers a different baked item. Each chapter begins with a brief, general discussion about the item. This is followed by a grouping of the problems that may occur according to the stage at which you are working. When you are interested in a particular problem mixing cookies, for example, you may turn to the chapter and study the section about mixing cookies.

The appendix of **BAKING SOLUTIONS** is packed full of exceptional information in a framework of text and convenient conversions. Whether you are experienced or just becoming familiar with home baking, this vital information will make your project run smoother.

SOLUTIONS

Question: *My family demands a consistent look and taste in the baked treats I produce, but no matter what I do, I have problems satisfying them. What is the answer?*

CONSISTENCY is probably the most important word used in baking language. The authors' focus is totally directed to making your baking, whether from scratch, a pre-mix base, frozen, or ready-to-use products, consistent from day to day.

Question: *The picture with the recipe promised a gorgeous chocolate cake. However, my cake sank in the middle when I removed it from the oven. I followed the directions. What could have gone wrong?*

The recipe's directions should only be used as a guide to baking. **BAKING SOLUTIONS** tells you how to deal with the variables in your kitchen which may cause the recipe to be changed.

Question: *I like to make cream fillings from scratch, but I usually scorch the mix before it's done. What am I doing wrong?*

Technique is everything and scorching a cream filling is usually a technique problem. The ingredient list of your recipe should be thought of as building blocks. The method you use to assemble those blocks will determine how the final product will turn out.

BAKING SOLUTIONS tells you how to assemble ingredient lists so your success will be assured.

Question: *My cookies get as hard as rocks. Am I baking them too long?*

Often the obvious answer is not the correct answer. Sometimes there is more than one answer. **BAKING SOLUTIONS** tells you several possible answers to each of your problems. All you have to do is find the one(s) that fits your situation.

Question: *I like really moist cakes. Mine are usually dry or else they are rubbery. What must I do to make a moist cake time after time?*

This is usually a problem of environment and method. **BAKING SOLUTIONS** tells you how to deal with both.

Question: *My bread rolls are heavy and have a pale crust. It's my grandmother's recipe. How come her's was always good?*

Grandmother probably baked a lot. She had a special touch, gained from repetition. There is no substitute for repetition or for that special touch. **BAKING SOLUTIONS** is full of baking advice which will help you avoid trial and error baking. You'll probably never bake exactly like anyone else. **BAKING SOLUTIONS** will help you bake better.

These are just a few of the everyday encounters you may have with baking problems. In each of these examples solutions exist to solve the problem. But, if you don't understand the problem, you'll probably end up telling yourself that your failure was just an expensive and time consuming lesson. The tips, methods, and suggestions found in **BAKING SOLUTIONS** will answer many of your baking problems. The sooner you use it, the sooner you will experience baking success time after time.

WARNING—— DISCLAIMER

This book is designed to provide information in regard to the subject matter covered. It is not the purpose of this book to reprint all the information that is otherwise available to the authors and/or publisher, but to complement, amplify and supplement other texts. You are urged to read all the available material, learn as much as possible about baking and to tailor the information to your individual needs.

Learning to bake better is not a get-rich-quick scheme. Anyone who decides to learn baking must expect to invest a lot of time and effort.

Many people hold great pride in their baking accomplishments at home. This book will help them be more proficient in the baked items they make.

Every effort has been made to make this book as complete and accurate as possible. However, there may be mistakes both typographical and in content. Therefore, this text should be used only as a general guide and not as the ultimate source of learning more about baking.

The purpose of this book is to educate and entertain. The authors and Ycart Publishing shall have neither liability nor responsibility to any person or entity with respect to any loss or damage caused, or alleged to be caused, directly or indirectly by the information contained in this book.

If you do not wish to be bound by the above, you may return this book to the publisher for a full refund. Please write the publisher for details before returning the book.

Notice: *All brand names, trademarks and/or registered trademarks are used for identification purposes only and are property of their respective owners.*

Mixers

-Kenneth Power

I've used almost every kind of mixer made to mix different recipes. Some mixers have different speed settings telling you how fast it will run or what to mix at that setting. Some mixers have numbers that you set to mix slow or fast. Whatever the system your mixer uses to signify speed should be followed in the mixing stages of your recipe.

Failure to follow your mixers speed setting may result in a burned up motor or a ruined recipe. Most of the home type mixers I've used will just barely do the job of mixing cookie doughs. Bread doughs usually cause them more strain than they can handle. If you are a serious home baker it is a good idea to invest in a heavy duty mixer. These cost several hundred dollars, but will give a lifetime of service doing all your mixing tasks.

Measuring Ingredients

-Lyndal Power

Using cups and spoons to measure ingredients is about the most primitive method you can possibly use.

It is far better to buy a small scale and weigh the ingredients. Weighing will insure that you use exactly the same amount each time the recipe is made. The first time you make a recipe, convert it to ounces by weighing each ingredient as you use the spoons and cups. After that initial effort the recipe will be easily and exactly repeated by weighing out the ingredients. I use a digital scale that measures in tenths of an ounce and it is perfect.

Chapter

And

Biscuits

Contents

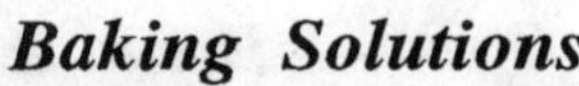

CHAPTER ONE

BREADS

NOTHING compares to the fresh baked aroma of bread and rolls. Setting your table with fresh baked bread will complement any meal and is certain to bring raves from family and friends.

Bread comes in just about as many shapes and flavors as there is ideas. It has been around for centuries. Its appeal remains as strong as ever. Where ever there is wheat grown—bread is baked and served as the mainstay of life.

Making bread from scratch is probably the most time consuming task of home baking. Bread baking is not hard to do, it just takes time. If you like to create unique flavors or like special health type bread, then scratch baking is the way to go. If you like the smell and taste of fresh baked bread, but don't want to spend the time making it from scratch, there are plenty of frozen breads you can bake. A boxed pre-mix of bread ingredients will still take a lot of time to prepare, but everything is pre-measured and ready to go.

Brouse through the following pages about bread making and you will see that it's not as hard as you may think. Have a little faith in yourself and soon you'll be baking bread quicker and better than Grand Ma's. You'll do it because you have better ingredients and tools to work with.

Professional bakers must always alter or add to their recipes with each change in their environment. A different oven, mixer, or even the time of year will cause a change in the way they make bread doughs.

You must also become aware of the variables of your kitchen environment in order to produce perfect yeast raised breads, doughnuts and sweet doughs.

Many people use pre-mixed ingredients and produce excellent bread. Others, who have less time, use frozen dough. Using pre-mixed ingredients saves a little time by eliminating having to measure ingredients. *However, all the other bread handling techniques are exactly the same as making from scratch.* When using a dough made from either a pre-mix or frozen you will find the methods of preparation, baking tips, finishing tips, and bread handling tips in this book to be of value.

"The most important thing to always remember is that your baking environment is different from anyone else's. Your oven will bake differently, your mixer will mix differently, the temperature of the pre-mix ingredients or your fresh ingredients will be different. Even the humidity of your kitchen will be different. You are unique and because of your being unique, the problems you face will be different from anyone else's."

TOOLS YOU WILL NEED

- A powerful mixer and attachment.
- A large bowl for holding the dough.
- An oven thermometer.
- A clean work space.
- A place at about 80 degrees for the bread to rise.
- A sharp knife to cut the bread.
- A spray bottle to hold water.
- A pastry brush to paint washes on the bread.
- Heavy cloth to remove the bread from the oven.
- Pans for breads and rolls.
- A wire rack to cool the bread.
- A pan release spray that does not contain flour.
- Measuring cups and spoons.
- A note pad and pen.
- If you are a serious bread maker, you must keep notes of your technique. Bread making is extremely variable, but can be done correctly time after time simply by paying attention to the environment.

- The best investment a serious home baker can make is to buy a small scale. It is far better to weigh the ingredients than to measure them. The scale should have a top weight of one pound and with it you can weigh fractions of ounces.

HINTS FOR BREADS

MIXING BREAD

- Make sure all the equipment is clean.
- Use the proper mixer attachment for mixing bread dough.
- All the ingredients should be cool when possible. The water should be cool or very cold (in the summer months). When using a pre-mix use the recommended water temperature.
- Prepare a place for the dough to rise in bulk before making it into loaves. This place should be draft free and about 80 degrees.

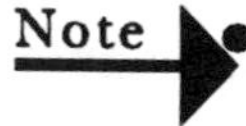

- Pay special attention to mixing times, so that the dough does not get too hot.
- If the mixer gets hot or pulls down, knead the dough by hand for the required time.
- Add salt about half way through the mixing time.
- When the dough is unusually wet and sticky, add more flour (a little at a time) until the dough is right.
- When the dough is unusually dry at the beginning of the mixing time, add a little more cool water.

Remember, all types of bread doughs have different characteristics. Some will be wet and sticky, while others will be dry. Your baking experience will teach you which is right.

- Add nut-meats, fruit, raisins, dates, etc. at the very end of your mixing time. Kneading them into the dough by hand is recommended.
- After mixing, place the bread in a lightly oiled bowl. Cover the bowl with a damp cloth or paper towel to protect the dough from drafts.

Special Note: *Please read the MIXING STEPS page at the end of this chapter.*

BAKING BREAD

- Pre-set the oven about twenty minutes before baking. When the oven reaches the pre-set temperature, use an oven thermometer to make sure the setting is correct.
- Season all new baking pans by applying a very thin coat of vegetable oil and baking them empty for about 25 minutes at 400 degrees. Cool completely, wipe dry and LIGHTLY grease them with all-purpose shortening before using.
- When using a spray release agent on the pans, make sure that for breads, the release agent does NOT contain flour. A very thin coating of all-purpose shortening (hydrogenated) will cause bread to release.

Note →

- Heavy steel pans are best for baking bread. Light weight pans may cause the crust to brown before the middle is done.

- Breads that contain sugar and milk will brown quickly, sometimes before they are done. Place a piece of brown paper on their tops about half-way through the baking time.

- Bread will bake fine at 350 to 410 degrees. Make sure the oven temperature setting is correct. Bread rolls always bake at a higher temperature than loaves (usually about 10 degrees).

- Hearth type breads like French bread and rolls should be cut before they rise to size. If you wait, they will be extremely fragile and may fall. Make the cuts about one forth of an inch deep from side to side inorder to insure good expansion in the oven and a pretty loaf.

- Brush on a wash of a fresh whole egg, mixed with a pinch of salt to make the crust shine. Brush this mixture on all crusty type breads before you cut them. Do not let this wash get on the baking pan. Egg wash will cause bread to stick to the pan. Brush a wash of oil or water onto pan breads.

- Brush on water when you wish to sprinkle on a topping. Brush on oil to make the top crust tender. Brush on before the bread rises and do not let the wash get on the baking pan.

- Do not let bread rise in a draft. The dough

will form a crust that will split and may cause small loaves, and will surely cause ugly loaves.

- Let all bread dough rise, before forming, to about 2/3 its desired finished size. Cover the bowl with a wet cloth or a damp paper towel while rising.

- Bread doughs should be kept at a room temperature of about 80 degrees while rising. Cooler temperature will make the dough take longer to rise. Warmer temperature will cause the dough to rise too quickly. A few degrees one way or the other won't matter.

Note →

- Use a hand spray bottle filled with water to spray a mist into the oven just before putting in the loaves. Crusty type breads like French bread should be sprayed as soon as you place them in the oven and again about 10 minutes later. They will have better expansion and a crispy golden crust.

- Bake rolls at a higher temperature than loaves, even when using the same dough for each. The smaller roll needs a higher temperature to avoid being dry.

- When bread loaves or rolls rise too much—don't dismay, just reform the dough again and let it rise to the correct size.

- When the dough feels too warm, place it, pan and all, covered in the refrigerator for about 15 minutes. After taking it out, allow the dough to rise the way you like and bake as usual.

- Brush the tops of brown-and-serve rolls with melted butter or margarine before baking and again as soon as you take them from the oven. The flavor and crust color will be better.

- Yeast dies at 140 degrees. Brown and serve rolls and bread must reach an internal temperature of 140 degrees in the oven to stop yeast action.

HANDLING BREAD

- Remove from the pans as soon as possible after baking and place them (*out of a draft*) on a cake rack.

- Place bread in plastic bags only after cooling completely. Warm bread will sweat and mold quickly.

- Freeze bread as soon as it is cool. Always put it in plastic bags, foil or wrapped inside a plastic box.

- All equipment should be clean to avoid mold.

- Rolls may be frozen, but only if they have gone through a correct packaging procedure.

Special Note: (*Rolls must be made and frozen in plastic bags as quickly as possible.*)

SOLUTIONS

QUESTION: *What is the best way to bake ready-to-use brown and serve rolls?*

First, brush their tops with melted butter or margarine. Bake at the recommended temperature (on their package), but be careful of dark coated baking sheets. Dark coated baking sheets may cause the bottoms to burn before they are done. Bake brown and serve rolls at a high temperature to insure a crispy, flavorful crust.

QUESTION: *Why are my breads always too hard and heavy no matter how I bake them?*

Breads made from scratch, a mix, or frozen, must have an internal temperature of about 80 degrees for the yeast to work properly. Cold dough will not expand properly. Make sure the bread rises in a warm draft free environment.

QUESTION: *Why does my bread rise too fast in the pan?*

Use cool or cold water in the mix. The place you let the bread rise in bulk should be about 80 degrees. Put the dough into the refrigerator for a few minutes to cool down (while the dough is still in bulk form).

QUESTION: *Why does my French bread have a pale crust?*

1. Spray or paint the loaves with water (before

cutting). Use an egg wash to make the crust really brown up.

2. French bread must have a high temperature to bake properly. Check the oven to make sure the temperature is correct.

3. Add a little sugar or milk powder to the mix.

QUESTION: *Why is my pizza crust tough?*

Most of the time a pizza crust dough should be wet and sticky (*use a little extra water*) to keep it from being tough. Toss in plenty of spices. Oil your pan with olive oil. Try baking the crust first, then add any topping and bake only to melt the cheese. Try dipping your fingers in olive oil when you flatten the crust in the pan. Use plenty of olive oil and the crust will be flavorful and crispy.

QUESTION: *Why are my bread loaves and rolls heavy and soggy in the middle?*

When everything else has been done right, maybe the bread's raw dough weight is too heavy. Try making the pieces smaller and let them rise longer.

QUESTION: *Why do my bread loaves cave in on their sides when removed from the pan?*

Always remove bread from the pan as soon as it is taken from the oven. The crust sweats if left in the pan and may cause the loaf to fall. Make sure that you use bread flour in the mix. Weak flour will cause loaves to fall. Make sure the loaves are done. Thump the top and if the loaf sounds hollow—it is done. Setting (just baked) loaves in a cool draft of air will sometimes cause their sides to cave in. When the dough is allowed to rise too much before baking the loaves will sometimes collapse.

QUESTION: *Is it all right to use Oatmeal or Oatbran in my bread mix?*

Sure—Oatbran may be added with the flour, but add Oatmeal about half way through the mixing cycle. Do not use instant Oatmeal. Instant Oatmeal will dissolve and change the bread's chemistry. Try substituting some of the water with apple sauce and use a little cinnamon in the mix when making Oatmeal bread.

QUESTION: *Why are my crusty breads always too soft?*

The secret to good crusty breads is to use very little (if any) fats, egg yolks, milks or sugar in the mix. Always serve crusty breads as soon as they are baked for the best flavor and appearance. Use only Bread Flour and make sure the dough is on the stiff side rather than soft and sticky. However, some crusty breads are very sticky (excess water). These breads are made by using an extra warm dough and baking quickly at a high temperature.

QUESTION: *How do I make loaves and rolls have a shiny crust?*

Wash their tops with a whole fresh egg mixed with a pinch of salt. This may cause the top to brown too quickly, so wash the loaves about 3/4 of the way through their baking time. Rolls can either be dipped or sprayed with evaporated milk. This will cause their tops to shine.

QUESTION: *Is it all right to freeze my breads and rolls?*

Yes. Freezing is the best way to keep breads and rolls fresh. Always freeze breads and rolls even when keeping them for only a few days.

QUESTION: *What should I use to keep my breads from molding?*

Nothing, unless you use a propionate in the mix. Always use clean equipment and pans. Cool bread quickly in a draft free place. Freeze breads to keep them and mold will never be a problem.

QUESTION: *Why didn't my bread rise in my bread making machine? I measured the ingredients correctly.*

ANSWER: Bread making machines are truly wonderful tools for the home baker, if you follow all the instructions to the letter. However, as in the old fashion way—sometimes changes must be made to make good bread. Yeast must be **fresh** and measured exactly. Some flour requires more liquid than other types of flour and you have to add more than the recipe calls for. The water temperature is very important to make the yeast active—too hot will kill the yeast and too cold will retard its action. Many variables are always involved in baking so it is a good idea to experiment and make notes of what you do. If the bread is perfect, you can repeat it time after time, but if it is not as you like, then you have to make changes.

TIPS ON DIFFERENT TYPES OF BREAD

FRENCH BREAD

French bread is probably the most popular crusty bread. Its characteristics are a fairly dense, chewy center surrounded by a golden brown crispy crust. French bread dough may be shaped into a loaf, thin stick, or a roll. The flavor is usually rather bland and is best when eaten very fresh and hot. French bread serves as an excellent complement for soups, salads, red meat and of course, all kinds of pasta dishes.

FRENCH BREAD TIPS

- ❖ Wash the tops of French bread with a mixture of one tablespoon salt and one cup water. Wash before the bread rises and then bake at 425 degrees for 15 minutes. At this time, wash with the salt water mixture again and turn the temperature down to 375 degrees. Let bake for 10 minutes and wash with the salt water mixture again. Continue to bake until done. This will give your French bread a very crispy and flavorful crust.

NOTE: *Let raw, bread dough thaw before brushing with the salt water mixture.*

- ❖ Slice baked French bread loaves, sticks or rolls and spread on a mixture of butter/garlic salt—*broil until crispy.*

- ❖ Cover with a dry paper towel and use your microwave for a soft bread.
- ❖ Grill in your oven's broiler, cut side up, for a crispy bread.

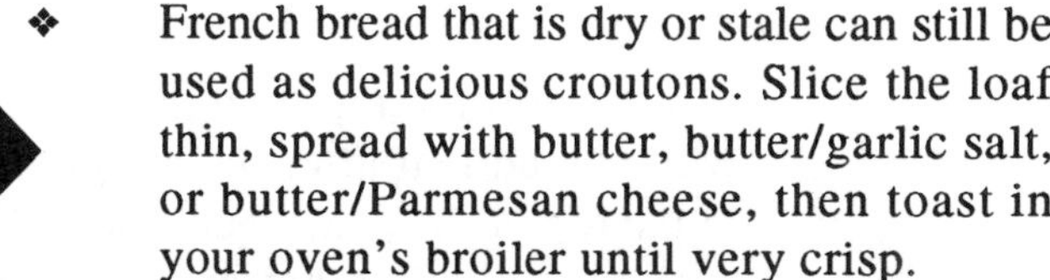

- ❖ **Note** French bread that is dry or stale can still be used as delicious croutons. Slice the loaf thin, spread with butter, butter/garlic salt, or butter/Parmesan cheese, then toast in your oven's broiler until very crisp.

WHITE PAN BREAD, LOAVES, ROLLS

White bread, Egg bread, Milk bread are types of bread that are usually baked in heavy steel pans however, thick glass pans will do. They are shaped into loaves, sliced thin and best suited for sandwiches. White bread's characteristic soft texture and thin crust lends itself to making a variety of small soft dinner rolls.

White bread is usually a flavorful bread that is on the sweet side with a slight egg taste. White bread complements fish dishes and cold cuts. In the shape of a roll, it goes with about any meal.

TIPS ON WHITE BREAD

- ❖ Brush melted butter on the tops of bread loaves and rolls as soon as they are removed from the oven. This will greatly enhance their flavor.
- ❖ Since white bread rolls bake quickly, dip them in evaporated milk before they rise for baking. This milk dip will give your rolls, whether made from scratch or bought frozen, a rich brown crust.

- ❖ For a different look and taste, follow the milk dip by sprinkling the rolls with poppy or sesame seeds. Do not wash white bread loaves with evaporated milk. The rich dough will brown quickly, but will not bake enough in the center.

- ❖ Gently split the top, length-wise, of your white bread loaf after the dough has risen to the top of the pan. Pour—don't brush—a trickle of melted butter or margarine in the cut. This will give your loaves a richer taste.

- ❖ Add raisins and a little cinnamon to the white bread dough. Make up the bread as usual for a delicious raisin bread. Spread a water/powdered sugar icing on top after the loaves cool.

- ❖ Flatten your white bread dough in the shape of a rectangle and wash with evaporated milk. Liberally sprinkle on a mixture of cinnamon/ground red cinnamon candy/granulated sugar. (Grind up red cinnamon flavored candies in your blender before mixing with the cinnamon and granulated sugar.) Carefully roll the dough into a loaf and place in your baking pan. Let the bread rise a little over the top of the pan before baking. After the bread cools, spread a water/powdered sugar icing on top of the loaf.

RYE AND PUMPERNICKEL BREAD

Rye and Pumpernickel bread are German breads. They are best suited for cold-cuts, cheeses and sausage. Their characteristics are, a soft crust and a firm texture that has a deliciously sweet aroma. Known for their keeping qualities, some say they even improve with age when wrapped in foil and stored. Rye bread can be baked in a pan, in a long loaf, or shaped in a ball. Pumpernickel bread is usually baked in a bread pan, although it's sometimes baked in the shape of a ball on a sheet pan.

TIPS ON RYE & PUMPERNICKEL BREAD

- Rye and Pumpernickel bread are both very slow risers. Always let them have plenty of time to rise before baking. The most common mistake is to put them in the oven too soon. This causes the loaves to be excessively heavy.
- Wash Rye bread with a mixture of whole egg/salt after the loaf has completed about three fourths of the baking time. This will give the bread a shiny crust.

- Following the suggested mixing times and methods is very important in making Rye and Pumpernickel bread. Their flavor depends on the proper aging of ingredients.
- Use a broom straw (real or plastic) and gently punch tiny holes in the Rye and Pumpernickel bread after the dough has risen to the top of the pan. This will make the dough stay flat on top and help the loaf maintain a fine grained texture.

Note: *Do not be rough or else the dough will fall.*

Rye and Pumpernickel breads have dominating flavors and are best eaten at room temperature. Spicy or sharp meats and cheeses are best, because they blend with the rye flavor enough to complement it.

ITALIAN BREADS

Italian breads are of two types. One type is like a French bread in that the loaf has a thick crispy crust with a full bodied center. This type of bread is usually made in loaves and rolls. The flavor of this bread is rather bland and complements soups, salads, pasta and dinner servings. As with all types of crusty bread, Italian bread is best if eaten very fresh and hot. The other type of Italian bread has a thin crust and an easy bite. This type of bread is used for Pizza crust and sandwiches. This dough may be baked as a plain loaf or it may have all kinds of spices, onions and olives baked in.

TIPS ON ITALIAN BREAD

- Make up and baking of Italian crusty bread is almost the same as French bread. However, the Italian version is usually not shiny. The bread is dull in appearance with loose bread flour on its top and bottom.
- Yellow corn flour is the proper dusting flour for Italian breads, but corn flour is difficult to find, so use bread flour or corn meal instead.
- Ground Fennel is a great Italian flavor. Surprisingly many recipes do not call for Fennel. Add a little Fennel to your bread dough or pizza dough and see what a dif-

ference it makes.

- ❖ Use plenty of olive oil to grease your pizza pan. Use olive oil to brush on the top of Italian flat breads. Olive oil will flavor the crust and make it crispy.

OATMEAL BREAD

Oatmeal bread is a pan bread baked in a loaf. The loaf is good as a sandwich bread, but also is great as toast. Oatmeal bread's characteristics are a thin brown crust with a soft, but firm bodied center. Oatmeal bread is extremely nutritious and is excellent for children's snacks.

TIPS ON OATMEAL BREAD

- ❖ If you don't have a recipe for Oatmeal bread just use your best White bread recipe. Substitute Old Fashion Oatmeal for 10 to 15 percent of the flour. Substitute apple sauce for half the water or milk. Add a small amount of cinnamon for flavor.

- ❖ Brush the top of the loaf with water and sprinkle on some Oatmeal for a unique appearance.

- ❖ Add raisins to the dough and increase the nutritional value. Nut-meats may also be added for extra flavor.

CROISSANTS

Croissants originally were served as a light French breakfast roll. They are now used for sandwiches, but still add distinction to any meal, at any time of day. They are characterized by their thin crispy layers of buttery flavored crust. Croissants are difficult to make properly and are usually bought raw and frozen or pre-baked and frozen. Frozen raw triangles of croissant dough are also very popular because they can be filled with cheese, cold cuts, or chocolate before baking.

TIPS ON CROISSANTS

- ❖ Thaw raw frozen Croissants in a warm, draft free place until they have risen to almost their full size. Sometimes this may take many hours. Professionals sometimes let them rise over night.
- ❖ Brush croissants with an egg wash before they begin to rise.
- ❖ Bake Croissants at 425 degrees for 10 to 15 minutes. Do not under bake.
- ❖ When using frozen Croissant flat triangles, let them thaw only enough to bend, then add the filling and roll up into the Croissant shape. Do not let the dough completely thaw before rolling the dough into the crescent shape
- ❖ When making Croissants from scratch, pay attention to keeping the dough cold at all times. The most common mistake is letting the dough become warm. Use a mixture of half real butter and half shortening for Croissant roll-in. The roll-in must be cool.

BRIOCHES

Brioche bread is a slightly sweet French breakfast bread that is usually made into a distinctive little roll on top of a big roll shape. Brioche dough can be chilled, rolled thin and cut into triangles to make a Croissant shaped roll. Brioche dough can be used also as a crust for deep dish meat pies. Brioche dough is delicious made into a Pepper bread loaf.

TIPS ON BRIOCHE BREAD

- Brioche is the richest of all bread doughs. Rolls should be baked at 360 degrees.
- Bread loaves should never be baked higher than 350 degrees. Wash Brioche with an egg wash to make it shine. Do not let the wash get on the baking pan. Brioche is very fragile and will tear apart if the dough sticks to the baking pan.
- Add 'dustless' black pepper to the dough and form into a loaf shape to make Pepper bread. Wash the top of the Pepper bread loaf with egg wash, but be careful not to let the wash get on the baking pan. Let the dough rise to slightly over the top of the pan and bake at 350 degrees until done. Carefully remove the loaf from the pan and cool on a rack in a draft free place.
- Use melted butter to grease the muffin pans for Brioche rolls.

HAMBURGER BUNS

Hamburger buns are totally American in their origin. They have a thin crust with a firm, but easy biting center. Most of the time they have plain tops, but sesame seeds give them a unique flavor. Hamburger buns made commercially are excellent, but if you want to customize the taste, or size, it's best to make them from scratch.

TIPS ON HAMBURGER BUNS

- ❖ Use any White bread, Egg bread, or Milk bread recipe to make Hamburger buns. Any bread that makes good dinner rolls will also make good Hamburger buns. Make the dough on the soft side for buns. Let the Hamburger buns rise to almost full size. Then bake them at a high temperature — 425 degrees for about 10 minutes.
- ❖ Do not use any kind of wash on Hamburger buns. Turn the buns upside down for cooling as soon as they are removed from the oven.
- ❖ Mix finely chopped onion into the dough for a unique flavored Hamburger bun. Make half sized Hamburger buns and use sausage patties for the meat. Half sized Hamburgers are great for parties.
- ❖ Brush the dough very lightly with water if you want to sprinkle sesame seeds or poppy seeds on top to the buns.
- ❖ Dill seeds and chopped onions mixed together in the dough is also a different way to flavor Hamburger buns.

WHOLE-WHEAT BREAD

Whole-wheat or Grain bread is full of flavor as well as nutritional.

Whole-wheat bread is a pan bread, baked in a loaf. Rolls and buns are sometimes made of whole-wheat dough, but the texture is best suited for loaves. Sliced whole-wheat bread makes excellent sandwiches and is good served with many meals.

The best whole-wheat doughs are really a combination of whole-wheat flours, white bread flours and rye flours.

TIPS ON WHOLE-WHEAT BREAD

- Add raw sun-flower seeds to your whole-wheat bread dough. Sun-flower seeds have a nut like taste and are simply delicious in breads.
- Always let whole-wheat bread dough rise to the top of the baking pan. Whole-wheat dough will not spring much in the oven.
- Use the handle of a wooden spoon to push at least four holes in your loaf of whole-wheat bread. Push the holes (from the top to the bottom) in the loaves before letting the dough rise. This will insure proper texture.
- Wash the top of your whole-wheat bread with salad oil before letting the dough rise. This will keep the top crust tender. Remove the loaves from their pans as soon as they are taken from the oven. Let the loaves completely cool on a wire rack before slicing.

BREAD FINISHING AND STORING

- Wash the top of hot freshly baked bread with melted butter or margarine. The crust will be softer and full of flavor.
- Cool bread as quickly as possible, on raised wire racks. Always avoid sitting loaves in a draft.
- **Note** → Remove bread from the baking pan immediately upon taking it from the oven. Bread rolls are best if they are removed from the oven when the crust is very light brown. Finish baking them just before serving.
- Freeze bread loaves and rolls as soon as they are cool. Freezing is the best way to store breads, if you want to keep them for a long time. Wrap tightly in plastic or foil.

A QUICK TOUR OF BREAD FAULTS

EXTERNAL APPEARANCE

Crust too dark — Causes

1. Your oven temperature was too high.
2. The recipe has excessive milk or sugar.
3. The bread has been over-baked.
4. The bread sat too long before baking.

Crust too light — Causes

1. Your oven temperature was too low.
2. The recipe has insufficient milk or sugar.
3. The bread has been under-baked.
4. The bread did not rise long enough.
5. The bread was not mixed enough.

Crust Broken — Causes

1. The bread did not rise enough.
2. There was not enough liquid in the recipe.

Crust too hard — Causes

1. Your oven temperature was too high.
2. The bread did not rise enough.
3. There was not enough sugar or shortening in the recipe.

4. Too much steam during baking.
5. Not enough liquid in the recipe.
6. The bread was baked too long.

Crust too soft — Causes

1. Your oven temperature was too low.
2. Too much sugar/egg yolks/shortening.
3. Too much oil/margarine used as a wash.
4. Not enough steam during baking.
5. The baking time was too short.

INTERNAL APPEARANCE

Poor flavor — Causes

1. Your dough was over-mixed and hot.
2. Not enough resting time before making into loaves.

Poor texture — Causes

1. You used a weak type of flour (cake or pastry).
2. Not enough resting time before making into loaves.
3. Not enough rising time before baking.
4. Not enough mixing time.
5. Over-mixing and the dough gets too hot.

INGREDIENTS FOR BREAD BAKING

FLOUR: Use only flour that is labeled BREAD FLOUR. All-purpose flour will make rich bread rolls, but will not give good results with loaves. Any crusty type breads, such as French bread, MUST have bread flour to make a correct loaf or roll.

SUGAR: Use honey, granulated sugar, corn syrup or molasses to sweeten bread. A little sweetener will act as a food for yeast and give bread greater volume. Sugar will also cause bread to brown quickly. Use small amounts of sweetener in crusty type breads.

MILK: Milk or milk powder will give bread flavor, act as a yeast food (milk contains a form of sugar) and cause bread to brown quickly. Use small amounts of milk in crusty type breads.

YEAST: Yeast comes in active, dry and dry instant forms. All are good to use in your breads. Active yeast must be fresh. When active yeast is gray or feels like putty, throw it away. Dry yeast must be dissolved in warm water before use. Dry instant yeast (best) can be added to your mix and no special care is necessary. Be sure to read the label on dry yeast to learn if it is instant and check the date for freshness.

SHORTENING: All-purpose shortening (HYDROGENATED) is best to use in bread. You may use margarine, butter, salad oil or olive oil, but because they have different effects on breads use them carefully. Use very little shortening in crusty type breads. Shortening will make them soft.

SALT: Salt is an important flavor ingredient in breads. It toughens the dough so use only a little.

WATER: Water should always be cool. In the summer months, water should be very cold. Usually the other ingredients will be at room temperature and they may be warmer than desired. Ice cold water will keep the dough from overheating while mixing.

NUTS: Nut-meats, raisins, dates, seeds, etc. should be added to the dough after it has finished mixing. Kneading nut-meats into the dough by hand is best. Whole wheat germ and bran can be added with the flour.

EGGS: Use whole fresh eggs in most type breads, however in crusty type breads use only egg whites. Egg yolks contain a high percentage of fat and will cause crusty type breads to be soft. Eggs should always be fresh. The egg's size is very important. When the recipe doesn't say—use large eggs.

LEMON JUICE: Lemon juice in very small amounts will give breads a slightly sour taste. This is especially good in French bread and rolls. Add a little lemon juice with the water.

OLIVE OIL: Use Olive oil to grease your pans. Lightly coat the inside of the baking pan and then wash the top of the loaf with olive oil.

ONIONS: Dehydrated onions are great to use in bread rolls. Add warm water and let them plump, then drain off the excess water and knead them into your favorite dough.

CHEESE: Parmesan cheese and garlic salt is very good sprinkled on the top of French bread sticks.

PEPPER: Use (dustless) black pepper when your recipe calls for black pepper.

SPICE: Use Rosemary, Oregano leaves and Fennel seed (whole or ground) for Italian breads or pizza crust.

BREADS AND YOUR MICROWAVE

- ☞ When reheating, the centers will be hotter than the outside, since the center contains more moisture.
- ☞ Over-cooking can make breads tough and rubbery. Breads should be reheated on a paper napkin or towel to absorb moisture. Reheat breads on ROAST setting. Eight ounces of rolls will reheat in approximately one minute, and fifteen seconds.

- ☞ Frozen breads may be defrosted and heated on SIMMER. Breads defrost quickly and easily on SIMMER. Always wrap them in a paper towel or napkin.
- ☞ If you use a microwave for baking breads, use ROAST or SIMMER setting. The texture and volume will be better.
- ☞ Usually you will not cover breads when baking. Leaving uncovered prevents the surface from being too moist.
- ☞ When baking in a microwave, the surface of breads will not brown. Doneness cannot be based on appearance. Place in a hot (pre-heated) conventional oven for a few minutes to brown the crust.
- ☞ Opening the microwave door while baking will not cause the breads to fall as it may in a conventional oven.

- ☞ Breads continue to bake after removing from the microwave and will be slightly damp when removed. They may also pull away from the sides of the baking dish.

- ☞ Cool loaf breads about 10 to 15 minutes in the baking dish.

- ☞ Freshen up day old or slightly dry rolls or breads by heating for a few seconds on ROAST. Place them on a paper towel while heating.

- Note ☞ NEVER USE METAL OF ANY KIND AS A BAKING PAN OR WRAP INSIDE YOUR MICROWAVE OVEN. Damage will occur.

BREAD MIXING STEPS

1. Use the attachment for mixing doughs on the mixer.

2. Mix the yeast (dry, instant or fresh) with luke warm water until it is dissolved.

3. Add the flour, water, shortening (or oil), sugar (or honey), milk powder, eggs and any other ingredients. Mix on low speed until everything is incorporated.

4. **Note →** At this point; if the mix is very dry and hard—add more water or egg yolk. If the mix is very wet and sticky—add small amounts of flour while mixing in low speed until the dough seems dry enough to mix properly. This stage must be done by sight and feel. If you plan on making this bread in the future—make notes of how much water or flour you have added to the recipe.

5. Mix for the amount of time written into the recipe. The dough should feel slightly warm (about 80 degrees). Buy a dough thermometer to know for sure.

6. Pull off a small piece of dough and stretch it between your thumb and finger—four ways. The dough should stretch into a thin membrane without breaking.

7. Place the dough in a draft free place (80 degrees) to rise before making it into loaves and rolls.

FINDING TOOLS

Finding the proper pans, mixer, cutters, thermometers, and other tools for bread making is sometimes a chore.

Try looking for a bakery or restaurant supply company in your city. They will sell to the public and offer all the tools you could ask for to make bread at home. Make sure that the larger pans will fit inside your oven before you buy them. Also ask if they have *used equipment.* You can make some super buys on pre-used bread pans.

Supermarkets sell BREAD FLOUR, but if your recipe calls for a type of flour not available; ask at your local bakery if they would sell you a couple of pounds. Bakers are good people and will usually sell you the flour (or whatever) and give you free advice as well.

BISCUITS

Making biscuits from scratch is quick and easy. Biscuits from a premix is convenient and you can customize the taste and size. No matter how you make biscuits, the method used to prepare and bake them is most important.

Many people make biscuits from pre-mixed ingredients which will produce excellent biscuits. When using a batter made from a pre-mix or frozen you will find the following methods of preparation, baking tips, finishing tips, and biscuit handling tips to be of value.

Using pre-mixed ingredients saves a little time and reduces the needed skill level as far as scaling and mixing goes. However, *all the other parts of biscuit handling is exactly the same as making from scratch.* Using these suggestions will save you time and money no matter which form of mixing you choose.

MIXING BISCUITS

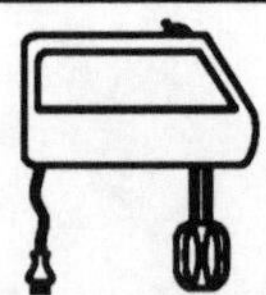

- Make sure all the ingredients are cool. The liquid must be cold. Mix the dry ingredients together, add the shortening and mix a little, then add the liquid and mix only until absorbed. Biscuit mix should be sticky and soft. Under-mixing is good, because handling the mix in final preparation will finish the job.

- Use biscuit pre-mix on the cutting surface to prevent the dough from sticking. All-purpose flour may also be used, but do not work the flour into the dough.

- Gently handle the scraps left after cutting. Work them back into a ball of dough by hand. This is a good time to work in a few raisins.
- Work quickly and keep the dough cold. If interrupted, place the cut biscuits and dough in the refrigerator until the job can be finished.
- Place the cut biscuits in the oven immediately (while they are cold). When you must wait, place them in the refrigerator until they are ready to be baked.

BAKING BISCUITS

- Pre-set the oven about twenty minutes before baking. When the oven reaches your pre-set temperature, use an oven thermometer and make sure the setting is correct.
- Season all new baking pans by applying a very thin coat of vegetable oil and baking them empty for about 25 minutes at 400 degrees. Cool them completely, wipe out the oil and LIGHTLY grease them with all-purpose shortening before using.
- When you use a spray release agent on the pans, make sure the spray does NOT contain flour. A very thin coating of all-pur-

pose shortening will also cause biscuits to release.

- Heavy steel pans are best for baking biscuits. Light weight pans may cause the crust to brown before the middle is done.

- Most ovens have a tendency to have hot spots. Avoid placing the pans at the back or near the sides of the oven. The middle of the center shelf is usually perfect.

- Biscuits must have a hot oven (385 degrees to 400 degrees) to bake properly.

- Place cut biscuits close together on the pan when you do not want their sides to brown. Place them at least one inch apart when you would like their sides to brown.

BISCUIT FINISHING AND STORING

- Brush the tops of the biscuits with melted butter or margarine before baking and as soon as they are removed from the oven. This will give a golden top crust with a super taste.
- When you feel like making sweet biscuits, try sprinkling brown sugar or maple sugar on their tops before baking.
- Place a small piece of pre-cooked ham or sausage inside each biscuit before baking.
- Glaze the biscuits with a mixture of honey and melted butter or honey flavored with preserves when you remove them from the oven.
- Note → Biscuits freeze well, but should be frozen as soon as possible after baking for best results. Bake them light, cool completely, wrap airtight and freeze. Do not thaw, just place the frozen biscuits in the oven and bake at a 350 degrees until the crust is perfect. Serve as usual.

SOLUTIONS

QUESTION: *Why are my biscuits heavy and hard?*

Heavy, hard biscuits are caused by over-mixing the dough. A low temperature while baking could be the cause. Old baking powder or letting the baking powder begin to work before putting the biscuits in the oven (letting the dough get warm), will also cause biscuits to be hard or heavy.

QUESTION: *Why is the crust on my biscuits pale when they are done?*

The oven temperature is too low. Try a higher setting. Brush the tops with melted butter or margarine before baking and again as soon as they are removed from the oven.

QUESTION: *Why do the bottoms of my biscuits burn before the tops are brown?*

Many ovens have excessive bottom heat. Using double baking sheets will prevent bottoms from burning when baking at very high temperatures.

QUESTION: *Is it possible to customize premade biscuits?*

Brush their tops with melted butter, sprinkle with sugar, add a small piece of pre-cooked ham or sausage before baking or glaze their tops with honey after removing from the oven. Sprinkle with bread type flour before baking for a homemade look.

QUESTION: *Why are my biscuits always over-mixed?*

Over-mixing is the most common mistake in making biscuits. Use very cold ingredients and stop mixing as soon as the liquid is incorporated into the mix. Handling during rolling out and cutting will finish the mixing process.

QUESTION: *Why do my biscuits bake unevenly, especially their tops?*

Usually the heat in the back of the oven is much hotter than by the door. Rotate the baking pan 380 degrees about halfway through the bake for more even top color.

TIPS ON PRE-MADE BISCUITS

- Roll each biscuit thin and place a small amount of thick fruit preserves in the center. Fold over to make a half circle (use a fork to seal the edges together). Fry (one side at a time) in a half inch of shortening, drain on a paper towel and sprinkle with granulated sugar. These quick fried pies are best when eaten right away.

- Brush the tops of your biscuits with melted margarine or butter. Brush one time before you bake, then again when you take them out of the oven.

- Flatten and place a piece of cooked sausage or ham across the middle then roll up and bake.

SCRATCH & BISCUIT MIXES

- Substitute one or two egg yolks for part of the milk or water added to the mix. When the mix calls for one egg, add one extra egg yolk. This will make a taster biscuit.

- Substitute milk for water or fresh cream for milk when you want pre-mix biscuits to taste more like scratch.

- Add raisins, cheese, orange peel, bits of chopped ham or pre-cooked bacon and sausage (crumbled and cold) to your mix for a new twist.

- Use a cookie cutter to make different shapes such as hearts, bears, etc.
- Dip your biscuit cutter into flour after each cut to keep it clean.
- Note → Use one level teaspoon of baking powder to each cup of flour when making scratch biscuits.

INGREDIENTS FOR BISCUITS

FLOUR: All-purpose flour is fine for biscuits. When bread flour is all you have, add one teaspoon of corn starch to each cup of flour. This will weaken the bread flour enough to make a tender biscuit.

BISCUIT PRE-MIX: Biscuit pre-mixes are very good. Follow the directions, but don't hesitate to make slight changes. The directions are only a guide. Your baking environment may make changes necessary.

WATER OR MILK: The water or milk you use must be cold. Biscuits rise because of the baking powder in them. Cold liquid will prevent rising action until they are put in the oven.

BAKING POWDER: Baking powder causes biscuits to rise. Baking powder must be fresh and kept cool during the mixing.

SALT: Use only a little salt. Salt will toughen the flour, but has a lot of influence on the biscuit's taste.

SHORTENING: All-purpose shortening, hydrogenated shortening, butter or margarine is fine to use in biscuits. A mixture of half butter and half all-purpose shortening is better. Let butter soften a little before using in the mix or combining with shortening. Shortening should be cool. Small lumps are desirable.

MILK POWDER: Milk powder will give biscuits flavor and cause them to brown quickly.

RAISINS: Add a few raisins to part of the mix (use scraps or divide the mix in half and gently fold in).

YEAST: Yeast is not usually used in biscuits. For a new taste try a little INSTANT dry yeast in the mix. Add the yeast at the beginning of mixing and follow the recipe as usual.

SUGAR: Granulated sugar, brown sugar, powdered sugar and maple sugar can be used in biscuits. Most biscuit recipes do not use sugar, but try a little for a different taste.

EGGS: Use fresh whole eggs as part of the liquid for a super tasting biscuit. Break a couple of eggs and place them in your measuring cup, add the liquid on top of the eggs to the correct level. This method will let the eggs replace a small volume of the liquid. Eggs should always be fresh. The egg's size is very important. When the recipe doesn't say — use large eggs.

CREAM: Use fresh cream instead of milk or water to make a richer biscuit.

There are lots of new and convenient premixed, frozen and ready-to-bake breads and rolls for you to try. Freshly baked bread has never been easier. The variety has never been better.
TIPS

Chapter 

CAKES

And

Frostings

Chapter Two——Cakes & Frostings

Contents

CHAPTER TWO

CAKES

A moist, beautifully frosted cake is the crown jewel of baking accomplishments. The art of baking perfect cakes is still the highest achievement of baking technique.

Combining the chemistry of raw ingredients to the correct balance, using the correct size container, and then adding just enough heat to bring forth an elegant creation is an art form in its own right.

This chapter will tell you many things to do and not to do when making cakes and frostings. We have successfully used these methods for many years and are sure they will help your home baking. It is a matter of learning a few rules in order to discipline yourself to the correct way of doing things. Cake making requires steadfast discipline, and rewards that discipline with an special treat.

Cake baking isn't difficult, it just demands close attention to each detail of the project.

Cake baking technique is not forgiving, when you make a mistake—the project is ruined.

Read the recipe's methods of ingredient combination carefully, think positively, throw in a handful of common sense and you will make perfectly baked cakes time after time.

Many home bakers make cake from pre-mixed

ingredients which will produce excellent cakes. Using pre-mixed ingredients saves a little time and reduces the needed skill level as far as weighing and mixing goes. However, *all the other parts of cake handling is exactly the same as making from scratch.* When using a batter made from a pre-mix you will find our methods of preparation, baking tips, icing tips, and cake handling tips to be of value.

TOOLS FOR CAKES AND FROSTINGS

- You'll need a good mixer and the proper mixing attachment for cakes and frostings.
- A rack for cooling the cake layers.
- Pans of various shapes and sizes. **NOTE:** Visit a restaurant /bakery supply house to find the kind of pans the pro's use. Ask about pre-used cake pans and sometimes you will find a good deal.
- Heavy cloth pads to remove the hot cake pans from the oven.
- A spray release that contains flour or use shortening and dust the cake pans with flour.
- A small scale to weigh the ingredients instead of measuring them. You have to convert the recipe to ounces, but you will be much more accurate time after time.
- A note pad and pen. Making notes of mixing, baking time and temperature and personal touch changes will insure repeatability.
- Cups and measuring spoons of the same size. Cups and measuring spoons of different brands will differ considerably in the amount they hold. Some are for measuring dry ingredients others are for liquids.

YOUR OVENS

Ovens have a tendency to have wide swings in the temperature they hold.

When they are heating up the temperature may rise several degrees past the setting. When they reach the setting—the heat source turns off. The time they are actually heating, at the required setting will vary with how well the oven is insulated.

Each time the oven automatically turns on and off signals a swing in temperature which is different from what you pre-set. A setting of 350, or 360, or 370 degrees may result in a perfect average between heating and cooling periods.

The way to know your oven's perfect average is to experiment. Experimenting is time consuming, but once you know—everything you bake will be better because of the effort. We have found that a baking temperature of 350 degrees is about perfect for almost all kinds of cakes.

Your Notes

MIXING STEPS

- Read and understand the recipe.
- Assemble the tools.
- Assemble the ingredients, making sure that they all are fresh and of the same BRAND NAME listed in the recipe.

- Follow the recipe directions to the letter as to the stages of mixing.

CAKE MIXING

- Use only fresh ingredients of the highest quality.
- Make sure all the mixing utensils are clean and cool.
- Use the beaters designed for cake mixing on your mixer.
- Make sure that all the measuring cups and spoons actually hold the same volume—when using more than one set. Fill one measuring cup up to the *one-cup* line then pour that water into the other measuring cup to make sure they both hold the same volume.
- Measure all ingredients as accurately as

possible.

- Always use ice cold water in the mix unless the directions or the recipe reads differently.
- Follow each step of the mixing procedure as faithfully as possible. Shortcuts almost always lead to disaster.
- Follow mixing times to the letter. Under or over mixing is probably the number one cause of cake failure.
- Angel food cake must be mixed and baked in a fat free environment. A drop or two of oil in the mix or on the cake pan will ruin the cake. Always invert Angel food cake as soon as the cake comes from the oven.
- Fill and place cake pans in the oven as soon as possible after mixing. Baking powder and baking soda start working as soon as they are added, so get the cake in the oven quickly.
- Use a rubber or soft plastic spatula to scrape the sides of the mixing bowl after each addition of ingredients. Scraping down the bowl is a must to insure proper ingredient distribution.
- Always cream the sugar and shortening/flour the correct amount of time. Good creaming will insure that plenty of air is added to the batter and that liquids will blend with the other ingredients.

BAKING CAKES

- Pre-set the oven about twenty minutes before baking. When the oven reaches the pre-set temperature, use a small oven thermometer to make sure the setting is correct.

- Season all new baking pans by applying a very thin coat of vegetable oil and baking them empty for about 25 minutes at 400 degrees. Cool completely, wipe dry, LIGHTLY grease them with all-purpose shortening and LIGHTLY dust them with flour before using.

- When using a spray release agent on pans, make sure that for cakes the spray DOES contain flour.

- When using a spray release agent on pans that does not contain flour, dust with flour after using the spray.

- Cakes that contain large percentages of sugar and milk will brown quickly. Bake this type of cake at a lower temperature than usual or cover with a sprayed/greased sheet of foil during the last few minutes of baking.

Note

- Most ovens have a tendency to bake hot or have hot spots. Consider using a slightly lower temperature than the recipe calls for when setting the oven.

- Baking pans that are coated with a dark

built-in release coating will sometimes burn cakes on their bottoms before they are done. Use a lower oven temperature when using this kind of pan or sit each pan on a baking sheet.

- Oven temperature is critical for cake baking. When possible—bake a small amount of cake batter in a cupcake liner when baking each particular cake the first time. A perfectly baked cupcake will usually mean that the temperature setting is correct.

- Most cakes should never be baked lower than 325 degrees and never higher than 375 degrees. A temperature setting of 350 degrees is a good place to start and if the oven is accurate, will probably do fine.

Note →

- Always use a pan of the proper size to bake cake. Check the recipe for the recommended size. The cake batter should fill the pan 1/2 full.

- Try to bake in the center (of the center rack) when possible.

- Do not let the cake pans touch each other or the sides of the oven.

- Do not open the oven door until the minimum baking time has passed.

- Test for doneness by inserting a wooden pick or wire cake tester in the center of the cake layer. If the pick is dry, remove the cake. If the pick is wet or sticky, let the cake bake for five more minutes then test again. An experienced baker can test for doneness by lightly touching the center of the layer. When the cake springs back to the touch, it is done.

- Let the cake layers cool five or ten minutes in the pans before inverting on a wire rack to finish cooling.

TIPS ON CAKES

1. Cake/Frosting combinations are endless. Bring them together the way you like and you can't go wrong.
2. Cool cake layers completely before icing.
3. Use a sharp knife and cut away humps and high sides. The layers should be fairly level before applying the frosting.
4. Cool cake layers completely in a draft free place, wrap air-tight and freeze for the best storage.
5. Do not unwrap the layers until they are completely thawed. Never ice layers until they have completely thawed.
6. Lightly brush any loose crumbs from the top and sides before icing.
7. When icing a cake, place the first layer {bottom side up} (add the frosting), then place the second layer {top side up} for a perfect match in the middle.
8. Make a small portion of frosting extra wet (add a little extra water). Ice the entire cake with a very thin coating of this wet frosting to set the crumbs and fill any gaps. Follow up by icing the cake as usual.
9. Buy a special icing spatula and use it to spread frosting on cake layers.

They will have a professional look.

10. Store cakes that have been iced with boiled type frosting under a cake dome that is lifted slightly by using a wooden pick. Don't plan on this type frosting lasting more than a day or two.
11. Store cakes that have been iced with a butter-cream type frosting under a sealed cake dome. They will last several days.
12. Brush (warm) uniced cake layers liberally with a hot simple syrup mixture or with hot jelly. Split thick layers and brush each one.
13. Use left-over frosting to ice cookies or place it between graham crackers. This makes a very simple treat that is hard to beat.
14. Remove the frosting from dry, left-over cake then cut the cake into small pieces. Place the pieces in a bowl and add a fruit flavored sauce or syrup to moisten. Mix together until the pieces are broken down and the mass is thick and sticky. Press this mixture on the bottom of a greased cake pan (about 1/4 inch thick). Add cake batter and bake as usual. Your next cake will have a pleasant surprise and there will be no left-overs.

SOLUTIONS

QUESTION: *Why does my cake batter run over the pan?*

Either the oven was set very low or you put too much batter in the pan.

Check the oven setting and never fill the baking pan more than 1/2 full of cake batter. Excess baking powder will cause the batter to run over the pan, so measure carefully.

QUESTION: *Why is my cake dry?*

The oven temperature was probably set too low and the cake dried out as it baked.

Cool cakes in a draft free area. They will dry out quickly in a draft.

QUESTION: *Why are my cakes soggy and fallen in the middle?*

The ingredients are out of proper balance. Make sure that you measure correctly. Excess shortening, liquid or sugar will cause this problem.

QUESTION: *Why are my cakes burned on one side?*

Improper placement in the oven will cause cakes to bake faster on one side.

Gently rotate the cake pans (don't pick up the pans—spin them) about 2/3 into the baking time for an even bake.

QUESTION: *What are the most common cake problems and causes?*

The following list covers just about all common cake problems and what caused them to happen.

EXTERNAL APPEARANCE

Crust too Dark — Causes

☞ Your oven was too hot.

☞ Your oven had too much top heat.

Cakes too Small — Causes

☞ Not enough batter in the pan.

☞ Your oven temperature was too high.

☞ Your batter temperature was too high.

☞ Your batter temperature was too low.

☞ You added an incorrect amount of water.

Cakes burnt on top — Causes

☞ Your oven temperature was too hot.

☞ You added an incorrect amount of water.

Crust too thick — Causes

☞ You baked the cake too long.

Cake falls during baking — Causes

☞ Jarring or moving the cake during baking.

☞ Your oven temperature was too low.

- ☞ You over-mixed the batter.

Cake shrinking — Causes

- ☞ The recipe has too much liquid.
- ☞ The batter was too cold.
- ☞ The oven was too hot.
- ☞ You did not follow correct mixing procedure.
- ☞ The cake was baked too long.

INTERNAL APPEARANCE

Coarse and Irregular Grain — Causes

- ☞ You used bad mixing procedures.
- ☞ Your batter was too stiff.
- ☞ Your batter was not level in the pans.
- ☞ Your oven was too cool, (baked too slowly).

Dense Grain — Causes

- ☞ Too much liquid in the batter.
- ☞ You did not mix correctly.

Off Color Cakes — Causes:

- ☞ You did not mix correctly.
- ☞ Your oven was too cool, (baked too slowly).
- ☞ You used unclean equipment.

GENERAL CAKE FAULTS

Poor flavor — Causes:

☞ You did not mix correctly.

☞ The shortening used to grease pans was rancid.

☞ Your cake was not baked soon after mixing.

☞ Your tools were not clean.

Cakes too Tough — Causes:

☞ You mixed too long.

☞ Not enough water in the recipe.

☞ Too much water in the recipe.

Lack of Body — Causes:

☞ You over-mixed the batter.

☞ Not enough water in the recipe.

Poor keeping Quality — Causes:

☞ Your cake was baked too long.

☞ Not enough water in the recipe.

☞ You did not mix correctly.

☞ Your cake was cooled in a draft.

HINTS FOR CAKES

BAKING

- Bake cakes at 350 to 360 degrees in regular oven. Bake cakes at 330 to 335 degrees in convection oven.
- Handle the cakes carefully when removing from the oven.
- Make sure the batter is level in the pans before baking.
- Cakes will spring back, when touched, when they are done.
- Baking time will vary with pan size and batter weight.

MIXING

- Batter temperature should be 70 to 75 degrees.
- ALL equipment should be clean and grease free.
- Pans should be greased properly.
- Use a paddle (not a wire whip) to mix the batter.
- Follow the formula exactly as to mixing

times. Add liquid to the mix in (stages).

- Always use fresh, high quality ingredients. Follow the formula exactly as to method.

HANDLING

- Turn hot cakes out gently on a wire rack.
- Cool completely in a draft free place—apply the icing or wrap for freezing.

How you handle a baked item is as important as what you put into it. Follow instructions!

TIPS ON SPECIFIC CAKES

YELLOW CAKE

Yellow cake is an old fashion cake that is noted for its moisture and flavor. Yellow cake has a fairly loose crumb and makes excellent layers, sheets and cupcakes. Yellow cake lends itself to be a perfect compliment for fruits such as strawberries and bananas. Yellow cake is also great with cream filling between the layers. Fresh fruit filling combined with a whipped cream frosting makes yellow cake a special treat.

TIPS ON YELLOW CAKE

- ✦ Oven temperature is critical for yellow cake baking. Make sure that the oven's internal temperature is correct.
- ✦ Chill fresh baked yellow cake in the refrigerator, then slice the layers in half. Make yellow layer cakes four thin layers instead of two thick ones. You can add more fruit or frosting and the cake will be more moist. Yellow cake dries out fast. (Note →)
- ✦ Let the layers cool in a draft free place and ice them as soon as possible.
- ✦ All-purpose flour is good to use in yellow cake when you plan to serve with fruit or cream filling.

✦ When yellow cake must stand alone with only frosting, then cake flour is best to use.

Note ➔

✦ Boxed yellow cake mixes are excellent. Add an extra egg yolk or a tablespoon of vegetable oil to give them a little extra moisture. Yellow cake is flavorful in itself, so use only a little vanilla extract in the mix.

HOLIDAY FRUITCAKE

Fruitcake is America's traditional Christmas gift. A good fruitcake has very little cake batter and is full of nuts and quality fruits. Fruitcake must be moist and must retain moisture. Fruitcake is traditionally baked in a ring form.

☺ Try heating commercially made fruitcake before serving. This will release some of the moisture collected in the dried/candied fruit.

TIPS ON FRUITCAKE

✦ Use only enough batter to hold the fruit and nuts together.

✦ Bake fruitcake at a low temperature—about 300 degrees for about an hour and twenty minutes. Cover the cake (brown paper) for the first forty-five minutes of baking time.

✦ Brush a honey or apricot glaze over the cake while it is still warm.

✦ Use only fresh candied fruit and fresh nuts in fruitcake.

- Do not plump raisins before adding to the mixture.

- After cooling—wrap and refrigerate or freeze fruitcake. Leaving it at room temperature will cause the nuts inside to become rancid.

- Try making fruitcake with all sorts of dried fruits. Use a good recipe for the batter and substitute different kinds of dried or candied fruits for the ones called for in the recipe.

ANGEL FOOD CAKES

Angel Food cake is the lightest of all cakes. They are low in calories and have no cholesterol. They are characteristically baked in a special ring Angel cake pan. Angel Food cakes lend themselves to being served with all sorts of fresh fruits. Strawberries, peaches, blueberries and cherries are deliciously complemented by Angel Food cake. A dollop of whipped cream makes fruit and Angel Food cake a very special dessert.

TIPS ON ANGEL FOOD CAKE

Note →

- Never spray or grease your Angle food cake pan. A tiny amount of shortening or salad oil in the baking pan or on any mixing utensils will bring disaster to your Angel Food cake. The mix will not tolerate any sort of oil. Anything that touches your Angel Food cake batter must be washed in hot soapy water, rinsed in hot clean water and thoroughly dried.

- Boxed Angel Food cake mixes are fair to good, but will always produce a different texture than an Angel Food cake made from scratch. Choose the way you like the best.

- Baking time is critical for Angel Food cakes. A little under-bake will cause the cake to pull itself from the sides of its baking pan and fall when removed from the oven.

- A little over-bake will cause the cake to stick fast to its pan and become tough. Bake Angel Food cake until the top is golden brown and is not sticky.

Note

- Always invert the Angel cake pan as soon as it is removed from the oven. A glass bottle makes a good stand to hold the Angel Food cake pan. If the cake touches a wire rack, it may fall. However, with some boxed cake mixes, cooling on a wire rack is fine.

- Add vanilla extract and a little almond extract to Angel Food cake batter. The almond extract will provide a good background flavor.

- Gently push down around the sides and stem of the Angel Food cake pan before tapping the cake out.

- If you like a darker crust on Angel Food cake, wet the Angel Food cake pan with cool water before filling with batter.

WHITE CAKE

White cake is the favorite cake for Birthdays, Weddings, and almost all special occasions. White cake is characterized by a very white crumb, tight grain and moisture. White cake's versatile form may include round layers, sheets, cupcakes and loaves. It is the best cake to bake in cake molds and is easy to frost and decorate. Its vanilla flavor blends well with almost all types of frosting.

TIPS ON WHITE CAKE

- Cream part of the cake flour with the shortening (one half or more of the required flour). This will make the cake hold moisture. Using all-purpose flour will cause white cake to be moist, but it will also have a clumpy grain and a slight off color. Using cake type flour is best for white cake. Cake flour will give it the proper grain and crumb color.
- Try using a 50/50 mixture of all-purpose flour and cake flour when making a white POUND cake. All-purpose flour will make white pound cake more moist and will give it a texture that will be acceptable for pound cake.
- Add a little almond extract along with vanilla extract. Use only a drop or two of almond extract because this extract is much stronger than vanilla and will make an excellent background flavor.

- Use cold water to mix white cake, whether using a box cake mix or from scratch. Proper texture and moisture retention depends on using cold water.

- When using a spray release agent on cake pans, make sure the spray DOES contain flour. When using a spray release agent that does NOT contain flour, dust the pans with flour after spraying.

- Baking temperature is critical for white cake. Pre-set the oven temperature about 20 minutes before baking. Make sure the oven's temperature setting reading is really the correct temperature. Large white cakes bake at about 350 degrees while smaller ones (such as cupcakes) should bake at about 365 degrees. Check the temperature with an oven thermometer.

Note

- Heavy steel or glass pans are best for baking white cake. Light weight pans may cause the crust to brown before the middle is done. Pans coated with a dark non-stick coating will bake faster than those without a coating or those with a light colored coating.

- Cakes that contain large percentages of sugar and milk will brown quickly. Bake this type of cake at a lower temperature than usual. Bake white cake at about 350 degrees.

- Remove white cake from the oven when the crust is golden brown and the cake's center springs back to the touch.

- Turn the cake out on a dusted (1/3 granulated sugar to 2/3 bread flour) paper as soon as they are removed from the oven. If the bottoms stick to the pan, bake for a few minutes longer. If the cakes are allowed to set in the pans too long, they may also stick to the bottom of the cake pan.

✦ Cool cake layers completely in a draft free place, wrap air-tight with foil or plastic wrap and freeze for the best storage.

Note → ✦ Do not unwrap the layers until they are completely thawed. Never ice layers until they have completely thawed.

✦ Large layers of white cake (for weddings, etc.) are best when left covered at a cool room temperature or placed in the refrigerator over-night. Icing them is much easier.

✦ Chill white cake before applying the frosting. Rub any loose crumbs from the chilled layers and trim the cake level. Place the cut sides DOWN as the layers are stacked.

✦ Brush room temperature un-iced cake layers liberally with a hot simple syrup mixture or with hot jelly to make them extremely moist tasting. Split thick layers.

✦ Make a small portion of the frosting extra wet (add a little extra water). Ice the entire cake with a very thin coating of this wet frosting to set the crumbs and fill any gaps. Follow up by icing the cake as usual.

✦ Store cakes that have been iced with boiled type frosting under a cake dome that is lifted slightly by using a wooden pick. Don't plan on this type frosting lasting more than a day or two. Store cakes that have been iced with a butter-cream type frosting under a sealed cake dome. They will last several days.

CHOCOLATE CAKE

Almost everyone loves some form of chocolate cake. Just hearing the words makes your mouth water for something sweet. Chocolate cake baking from scratch is fun, but with all the wonderfully delicious boxed cake mixes to choose from nothing could be quicker.

The two most common problems with chocolate type cakes are *under-mixing* and *over-baking*. Because chocolate is brown in color it is probably over-baked more than any other cake. Because of the high acid content of cocoa it is important to mix each stage exactly as the recipe is written.

TIPS ON CHOCOLATE CAKE

❖ Always follow the mixing directions on the package or on the box to the letter.

❖ Sift the cocoa and flour together to prevent lumps.

❖ Chocolate pound cake requires much more creaming of the sugar and butter than normal (sometimes as much as 10 minutes). If your chocolate pound cake falls when removed from the oven or has a very poor texture try mixing it one third longer than the recipe's directions.

❖ Carefully watch baking times and temperatures. It is far better for chocolate cake to have a slight under-bake.

❖ Remove the cake while it is very warm and cool quickly in a draft free place. Do not let stand uncovered at room temperature for any longer than possible. Chocolate cake dries out fast.

❖ Add a tablespoon of vegetable oil (with the liquid) to the recipe or cake mix and make the cake more moist.

❖ Chocolate cake will double in size so do not fill your baking pans more than 1/2 full of batter.

❖ Cut off the top crust of chocolate cake layers and liberally brush on a hot chocolate or rum flavored sauce.

❖ Make sure your oven is set at the right temperature for the size cake you are baking. Larger layers bake at a cooler temperature than small layers. A large sheet cake will bake at a 10 degree cooler temperature than regular 8 or 9 inch round cakes. If the cake peaks in the middle—the oven is too hot.

Note →

❖ Use a little orange flavored extract along with the usual amount of vanilla for a different taste treat.

❖ Never use old chocolate in your cakes or frosting. Chocolate absorbs odors and it will have an off flavor.

"Why not bake a chocolate cake today and serve it with home-made vanilla ice-cream?"

Chapter Two——Cakes & Frostings

CAKE AND FROSTING COMBINATIONS

WHITE CAKE

(Layers)

- ☆ Ice with White butter-cream.
- ☆ Ice with White butter-cream with chopped nuts on the sides.
- ☆ Ice with White butter-cream with fruit added; Banana, cherry, orange, strawberry, pineapple, raspberry.
- ☆ Ice with White butter-cream with flake coconut pressed on the top and sides.
- ☆ Ice with fruit jam such as cherry, apricot, pineapple, orange, raspberry, lemon; alone, or covered with nuts/ coconut.
- ☆ Ice with Chocolate butter-cream.
- ☆ Ice with Chocolate butter-cream on the sides with dark chocolate fondant type frosting on top.
- ☆ Ice with Chocolate butter-cream on the sides with fruit spread on top.
- ☆ Ice with Boiled frosting.
- ☆ Ice with Boiled Frosting and cover with coconut pressed on the top and sides.
- ☆ Ice with White Fondant type frosting alone or with flavors.

(Sheets and Cupcakes)

- ✩ Ice with butter-cream.
- ✩ Ice with butter-cream sprinkled with nuts/coconut.
- ✩ Ice with Chocolate butter-cream.
- ✩ Ice with Chocolate butter-cream sprinkled with nuts/coconut.
- ✩ Ice with White or Chocolate fondant type frosting, alone or with flavors.

DEVILS FOOD—CHOCOLATE CAKE

(Layers)

- ✩ Ice with White butter-cream.
- ✩ Ice with Chocolate butter-cream.
- ✩ Ice with Chocolate butter-cream with nuts pressed on the sides.
- ✩ Ice with Dark Chocolate butter-cream.
- ✩ Ice with Chocolate butter-cream on the sides and Dark Chocolate Fondant frosting on the top.
- ✩ Ice with White Boiled frosting.

(Sheets and Cupcakes)

- ✩ Ice with White butter-cream.
- ✩ Ice with Chocolate butter-cream.
- ✩ Ice with Chocolate butter-cream with nuts sprinkled on top.
- ✩ Ice with White Boiled frosting.

SPONGE CAKE *(Layers)*

- ✩ Ice with Lemon pie filling between

the layers and lemon fondant on the sides and top.

- ✩ Ice with Fruit jams; apricot, cherry, raspberry, apricot; between the layers and on top. Chopped nuts/coconut pressed around the sides.
- ✩ Ice with whipping cream, with Strawberry filling (fresh) between the layers.
- ✩ Place Vanilla Cream filling between a single split layer and Chocolate Cream filling on top.
- ✩ Ice the sides with Vanilla Cream filling and press on chopped nuts.

GERMAN CHOCOLATE CAKE *(Layers)*

- ✩ Ice with German Chocolate frosting.
- ✩ Ice with Dark Fudge, fondant frosting.
- ✩ Split the layers and place the frosting between them, on the sides, and on the top.
- ✩ Ice with White boiled frosting.

RED VELVET CAKE *(Layers)*

- ✩ Ice with Cream Cheese frosting.

CHOCOLATE RED VELVET CAKE

- ✩ Ice with German Chocolate frosting.
- ✩ Ice with Light Chocolate buttercream.
- ✩ Ice with Special (rich) chocolate frosting.
- ✩ Ice with Cream Cheese frosting with

chopped nuts pressed around the sides.

- ☆ Ice with White butter-cream and press coconut around the sides.

RUM CAKE *(Ring)*

- ☆ Dip in Rum Syrup.

(Loaf: Plain: Cupcakes)

- ☆ Ice with butter-cream, Chocolate, White, or colored white.

BANANA CAKE

- ☆ Ice with Banana flavored butter-cream and press pecan pieces on the sides.
- ☆ Place Vanilla custard with fresh sliced bananas between the layers.
- ☆ Ice with whipping cream. Sprinkle with Pecans.

ANGEL FOOD

- ☆ No frosting.
- ☆ Ice with Boiled frosting.
- ☆ Ice with Cherry flavored butter-cream, or Boiled frosting.
- ☆ Ice with Light Chocolate butter-cream and press chopped almonds on the sides.
- ☆ Ice with whipping cream to which you have added fresh chopped straw-berries, or peaches.

APPLE SAUCE CAKE

- ☆ Ice with Honey Spice frosting.

☆ Ice with Whipped Cream. Sprinkle chopped nuts on top.

☆ Ice with Chocolate butter-cream.

CHEESE CAKE

☆ Top with sour cream and sprinkle cinnamon.

☆ Top with fruit pie filling.

☆ Top with almond filling.

CHOCOLATE APPLE SAUCE CAKE

☆ Ice with white fondant type frosting.

CHOCOLATE CAKE

☆ Ice with chocolate or white butter-cream.

☆ Ice with chocolate flavored whipping cream and decorate with shaved chocolate and cherries.

☆ Ice with boiled frosting.

CHOCOLATE VELVET CAKE

☆ Ice with whipped cream and decorate with shaved chocolate.

GINGER BREAD CAKE

☆ Ice with Honey spice frosting.

☆ No frosting, just sprinkle with powdered sugar.

☆ Serve with whipping cream.

GOLD CAKE

☆ Ice with White butter-cream.

☆ Ice with Boiled frosting.

- ☆ Ice with Chocolate butter-cream.
- ☆ Ice with Whipping Cream.
- ☆ Ice with Honey Spice frosting.
- ☆ Decorate with chopped nuts, cherry halves, shaved chocolate, whole pecan halves, or flake coconut.

LEMON POUND CAKE

- ☆ No frosting, apply a sauce.
- ☆ Ice with Lemon fondant type frosting.

ORANGE CHIFFON CAKE

- ☆ Ice with Orange glaze.
- ☆ No frosting.
- ☆ Ice with orange flavored butter-cream.
- ☆ Ice with Chocolate glaze.

PUMPKIN CAKE

- ☆ Ice with Honey Spice frosting.

PECAN FUDGE CAKE

- ☆ Ice with Chocolate Fondant type frosting. Press pecan pieces on the sides.
- ☆ Ice with boiled frosting and sprinkle chopped nuts on the top.
- ☆ Ice with Chocolate butter-cream, Drizzle hot chocolate fondant over the top.

SPICE CAKE

- ☆ Ice with Honey Spice frosting. Decorate with chopped nuts.

CAKES AND YOUR MICROWAVE

The following tips will help you use the microwave for cakes.

- ❖ For best results, ingredients for cakes should be at room temperature, measured accurately, and the batter mixed and baked according to recipe directions.
- ❖ The simplest and easiest way to prepare cake dishes is to lightly grease the bottom and sides of the dish with vegetable shortening and lightly dust with flour. Waxed paper may be used to cover the bottom of the dish, making cakes easy to remove.

- ❖ Cake dishes should not be filled over half full. Microwaved cakes increase substantially in volume and the texture is somewhat lighter than conventionally baked cakes. Save the extra batter for cupcakes.
- ❖ Bake one layer at a time and allow each to cool no longer than five minutes before removing from the dish, unless otherwise noted in the recipe.
- ❖ Over-baked cakes will be dry and slightly hard or tough. It is always better to underbake and check for doneness frequently toward the end of the baking period.
- ❖ If you desire a cake with a heavier texture, place plastic wrap over the top of the cake batter.

- ❖ Most cakes are less porous in texture and give the best results when baked at about 70% power. This would be the ROAST setting on many microwaves.

- ❖ Commercially frozen layer cakes may be defrosted on SIMMER. A 16 ounce cake defrosts in one minute, fifteen seconds on SIMMER. Cakes defrost quickly and easily. Whole cakes will need a standing time to equalize temperature.

- ❖ The ideal utensil for baking cakes in your microwave oven is doughnut shaped. Plastic tube pans or ring molds designed for microwave baking, give excellent results.

> *"It's easy to over-bake things in your microwave. Follow the directions to the letter and don't over-do it."*

INGREDIENTS FOR CAKES

Each time we create a recipe we use specific ingredients. A specific kind (brand name or type) of sugar, shortening, flour, baking powder, soda, cocoa, etc. Because we use these specific ingredients in our recipe it will be the same time after time, if we continue to use the same ingredients. If we change to a different brand name or type, our recipe may require a slight alteration to compensate for the change.

When you are making an old family recipe the results may be different than expected because you will be using different brand names or types of ingredients from those used in the original recipe. We don't have an easy answer to this problem other than to experiment a little with different brand names or types of ingredients until you are able to duplicate the recipe. You still may never find the correct combination.

Grandma's chocolate cake was unique because her ingredients were unique to her time. They say our ingredients are better, improved, whatever, but one thing is for sure—they are different. Rather than trying to duplicate Grandma's cake it's far better to make a great cake by using the ingredients that are available to you today.

Some things are worth repeating and asking you to buy a small scale to weigh out your ingredients is one of them. Buy a scale that weighs in tenths of an ounce so your small ingredients will be weighed accurately. A digital scale is perfect for the job. The first time you make a recipe, measure the ingredients to the scale and make notes of each items weight. If the cake or whatever comes out perfect, use the weights you've written down to make the cake in the future. Measuring your ingredients with cups and spoons is just not accurate enough to make repeatability a sure thing.

SUGAR: Super fine or Fine granulated sugar is best for cakes.

SHORTENING: All-purpose shortening is good. Butter is good. Emulsified shortening is best. Emulsified shortening blends best with the sugar and holds moisture in the cake. Use emulsified shortening *ONLY* in cakes and icings. Emulsified shortening should never be used in other baked items or used to fry donuts. Ask your local bakery to sell you some emulsified shortening.

EGGS (Yolks): Always use fresh whole eggs. When you use yolks and not the egg white, bring to about 70 degrees by placing the eggs in water to warm and then separate them carefully. Always use large size eggs. HINT: If you measure eggs with 2 yolks to 1 white it will be a better cake.

COCOA: Cocoa will absorb odors. Make sure that the cocoa you use is fresh. Push through a sifter if lumpy.

BUTTER: Butter goes rancid quickly and will also pick up odors. Make sure that you only use fresh, tightly wrapped butter in your cake mix. Let the butter get a little soft before using, but do not let separate. Butter should be cool, but not cold when you blend with the other ingredients.

WATER: Use ice cold water in all your cake

mixing, whether from scratch or from a boxed premix. Ice cold water will keep the baking powder strong until the cake goes into the oven. Ice cold water will chill the shortening and keep the shortening from breaking down in the creaming process.

MILK: Milk and milk products give the cake flavor, cause the cake to brown and helps hold moisture. Use fresh milk, buttermilk and milk powder in your cake mixing.

OIL: Some recipes call for salad oil. You should always make sure the oil is fresh. All oil goes slightly rancid in time and will pick up odors.

VANILLA EXTRACT: Vanilla is the primary flavoring for cakes, use it fresh and of the highest quality.

ALMOND EXTRACT: Almond extract gives the taste of cherries. Use a LITTLE almond extract along with vanilla to perk up white cake and white frosting.

ORANGE EXTRACT: The taste of orange extract compliments chocolate perfectly. Add a LITTLE orange extract along with vanilla to perk up chocolate cake and chocolate icing.

NUT-MEATS: Nut-meats enhance all kinds of cakes, but always make sure they are fresh because they become rancid quickly.

FLAVORS: Flavor frosting the way you like. Most flavors are concentrated, so taste as you add and don't over-flavor.

CORN SYRUP: Use light corn syrup in both

butter-cream and boiled type icing. Corn syrup makes the frosting moist and shine.

EGGS (whites): Use the whites in meringue or frosting. Do not let part of the egg yolk get into the egg whites. Egg yolk contains a lot of fat and fat will cause angel food cake to collapse. Also, make sure the container you put the egg whites in is free from any form of fat, oil or shortening. Eggs should always be fresh. The egg's size is very important. When the recipe doesn't say—use large eggs.

FLOUR: Use cake flour in making almost all kinds of cakes. All-purpose flour is fine for some fruitcakes and pound cakes, but will cause most cakes to be grainy. When an all-purpose flour is all you have, try adding a level teaspoon of corn starch for each cup of all-purpose flour. The corn starch will weaken the flour enough to make a good cake. You can also substitute all-purpose flour for cake flour by using 2 tablespoons less per cup. (This is definitely not as good as using cake flour, but will do.)

SALT: Salt is an important flavor ingredient in cakes, but use only a small amount as it will toughen the flour.

BAKING SODA: Make sure that the baking soda is fresh. Baking soda picks up odors and will ruin the taste of your cake.

BAKING POWDER: Make sure that the baking powder is fresh. Baking powder loses strength with age and will ruin your cake. When in doubt — buy fresh.

CORN OIL MARGARINE, WHIPPED BUT-

TER, WHIPPED MARGARINE OR ANY LOW CALORIE MARGARINE: Never substitute these in your recipe. They require special recipe changes that takes a lot of experimenting.

COCONUT: Use fresh, moist coconut in your cake and frosting. Freshen up a package of dry coconut by putting with a few teaspoons of water in a jar and shaking. Toast it lightly for inside and out.

CAKE FROSTINGS

Making delicious frosting is a snap. Perfect frosting gives cakes, brownies and cookies the special fancy 'sizzle' that makes their eating irresistible.

BUTTER-CREAM frosting is a mixture of butter, margarine or shortening with powdered sugar. Water, milk, or egg whites are used to thin butter-cream. Chocolate and an endless number of flavors may be added to change butter-cream frosting to compliment any cake flavor.

BOILED frosting is a mixture of egg whites, granulated sugar, water and corn syrup. The sugar, water and syrup are brought to a boil, removed from the heat, and streamed into egg whites which are being whipped. The mixture is finally whipped to a thick meringue.

Boiled frosting must be whipped in an oil free environment. A single drop of oil in the mix or adhering to utensils will prevent the egg whites from whipping. Oil free flavors may be added.

FONDANT frosting is sugar based. It is very fine textured and usually must be heated or thinned down before use. Fondant frostings are noted for their shine, hard crust and versatility.

MIXING FROSTING

Any mixer will do for mixing frostings. Use the appropriate beaters. Make sure that all mixing utensils are spotlessly clean and oil free.

MIXING BUTTER-CREAM FROSTING

- Cream the powdered sugar (plus cocoa, if chocolate frosting) with the shortening, margarine, or butter until the mix is light and fluffy.
- Add the flavor and any liquid to the mix very slowly. Add only enough liquid to make the mix easy to spread. Use your judgement when adding liquids. Excessive liquid (sometime even flavor extracts) will cause the mix to separate.

Note →

- Add melted chocolate last and mix only enough to incorporate. The more the chocolate is mixed; the lighter in color the frosting will become. When the chocolate cools, the mix will become slightly thicker. Use this type of frosting as soon as possible.

MIXING BOILED FROSTING

There are two good methods for making boiled frosting.

- The first method requires placing all the ingredients in a double boiler and whipping as it heats (while over the hot water) until a stiff peak is formed.
- The second method is to bring the sugar, water and light corn syrup to a boil, then add the hot mixture (very slowly) to pre-whipped egg whites. The mixture is whipped on high speed to a firm peak as the hot liquid is being added.

Both methods will produce a good boiled frosting, so use the method you think is best for you.

- ❖ Do not over whip boiled frosting. If boiled frosting is over-mixed, too much air will be incorporated. The frosting will be thick, full of air holes and impossible to spread.

- ❖ Use boiled frosting as soon as possible after whipping. Boiled frosting sets up quickly and is almost impossible to spread after cooling.

- ❖ Sometimes (not always) it is possible to save an over mixed boiled frosting by putting it back into a double boiler and reheating, then re-mixing. It's worth trying.

Note →

MIXING FONDANT TYPE FROSTING

When making fondant frostings for cake, brownies and eclairs use fresh sifted powdered sugar when possible. Add a mixture of cool water, light corn syrup and flavor slowly to make a very thick, smooth paste. Heat the fondant to warm only before use. When using fondant as a cookie icing add less water. Heat the thick mixture to thin it for use. It will harden to a correct consistency when it cools on the cookie.

- ❖ Add any food coloring or flavor to fondant for seasonal cookies, brownies, donuts and cakes.

- ❖ We always pour a thin layer of vegetable oil over any fondant we're saving to prevent it from crusting over.

SOLUTIONS

QUESTION: *Why does my boiled frosting fail to come to a firm peak?*

Usually boiled frosting won't whip to a peak when there is even a minute amount of oil in the mix or on mixing utensils. Everything used to make boiled frosting must be spotless.

QUESTION: *Why is my boiled frosting difficult to spread?*

You probably have whipped it too long. When over mixing is the problem; slowly add a little light corn syrup (while mixing) and thin the icing down enough for easy spreading. A last resort would be to re-heat the mix and then try to whip it again. (Sometimes this won't work.)

QUESTION: *How do I keep crumbs from getting in my frosting when applying it to a cake?*

First of all, brush all the loose crumbs and edges from the cake layers. The frosting should be wet enough to spread on the cake without picking up crumbs. Use a icing spatula and start with a large lump of frosting and spread it thin.

If the cake is an opposite color, (chocolate cake/ white frosting) first thin a small portion of the frosting until it is very wet and apply a thin layer to the entire cake. This wet frosting will set the crumbs and fill cracks. Don't worry about crumbs getting into this layer of frosting Let the thin layer of frosting sit for a few minutes, then apply a thick layer of regular frosting over it.

QUESTION: *Why does my boiled frosting get thick and gummy after a few hours?*

You probably are over mixing and adding too much air to the frosting. Add an extra amount of light corn syrup to the frosting while mixing. Store any cake that has been iced with boiled frosting under a cake dome, but use a wooden pick under the lid to lift the dome up a little and allow a small amount of air in. Sitting a cake that has been iced with boiled frosting in a draft will cause the frosting to quickly become thick and gummy.

QUESTION: *Why does my butter-cream frosting taste gritty?*

You are probably using old powdered sugar or powdered sugar that has not been stored properly. Powdered sugar will pick up moisture from the air and will not cream properly with the shortening. Sifting the sugar will usually not stop the problem, so always use fresh powdered sugar and then store any left over in an air tight container. If butter-cream frosting is left to sit in a draft before using, it will form a thin crust. This crust will make the frosting taste gritty when it is mixed into the frosting and then used on the cake. Always cover the bowl holding the frosting with a damp cloth and a crust will not form.

QUESTION: *Why do I have small lumps of shortening in my butter-cream frosting?*

Creaming the powdered sugar and shortening thoroughly together is very important. Butter should always be softened to room temperature before creaming. Adding a liquid to thin the frosting before the shortening is completely creamed with the powdered sugar, may cause lumps. The resulting small shortening lumps are there to stay. Adding hot liquid will sometimes help the shortening cream better, but hot liquid also can cause the butter-cream to melt and separate. Add liquid slowly to the mix (as you mix) and lumps should not be a problem.

QUESTION: *Can I freeze a cake that has been iced?*

You can freeze a cake that has been iced with a butter-cream frosting. Freeze the cake (unwrapped) until it is solid. Then wrap with foil and place back in the freezer. Let the cake thaw in the refrigerator before unwrapping. A cake iced in a boiled type frosting will not freeze well. The frosting will be ruined if you try to freeze it.

QUESTION: *What is a good flavor combination for white butter-cream frosting?*

Try vanilla and a little almond extract. When using butter for the shortening, try vanilla and a little orange extract. Always use a small amount of any strong flavor as the background taste.

QUESTION: *I want a very dark chocolate frosting on top of my devil's food cake layers, but I want to use a lighter chocolate frosting for between the layers and outside edges. What must I do?*

You should use two types of frosting. For the top simply melt a small quantity of chocolate morsels along with a little heavy cream. Do not whip this mixture. Ice the sides and between the cake's layers with regular chocolate butter-cream, then carefully spread the warm, melted chocolate over the cake's top.

TIPS ON FROSTING

BUTTER-CREAM

- Mix cocoa/oil with the powdered sugar before creaming with shortening in butter-cream frosting. Mix three level tablespoons of cocoa with one tablespoon of salad oil or melted shortening to make one block (one ounce) of unsweetened baking chocolate. When making a portion of the butter-cream chocolate flavored, use the cocoa conversion to make the chocolate flavor. Do not add raw cocoa to the finished butter-cream frosting.

- Use Emulsified shortening when using food colors or colored jams in butter-cream frosting. Ask your local baker to sell you some.

- The more butter-cream frosting is mixed (after the chocolate has been added) the lighter in color the frosting will become. When you want a darker chocolate butter-cream, do not mix the frosting more than necessary to blend in the chocolate.

- Chill freshly baked chocolate cake layers in the refrigerator before applying the frosting. Gently rub any loose crumbs from the chilled layers and you will not have as much trouble spreading the frosting.

BOILED FROSTING

- ❖ A little Cream of Tartar mixed with the dry sugar (before cooking) will make firmer and whiter boiled frosting.
- ❖ Note ➔ Cool cake layers completely before icing. Use a sharp knife and cut away humps and high sides. The layers should be fairly level before applying the frosting.

FONDANT FROSTING

- ❖ Thin fondant frosting by heating or use a small amount of hot liquid. Hot coffee is excellent to use when thinning Chocolate fondant.
- ❖ Always keep fondant frosting covered with plastic or a thin layer of vegetable oil.
- ❖ Use a drop of colored fondant on a cookie. Sugar cookies look wonderful when dipped in thin fondant frosting. Children love the color and the extra sweetness.

USING AND STORING FROSTINGS

- Use the frosting as soon as it is made. All frosting sets up quickly and either forms a crust or becomes very stiff.
- Buy an icing spatula to apply frosting. A good icing spatula will enable you to work faster and the results will look great.
- Note → Apply fondant frosting to brownies while they are warm. The frosting will melt slightly and form a shiny surface. Sprinkle on nut-meats while the frosting is sticky and soft. When brownies are cold, warm the chocolate frosting (a little) in a double boiler or in your microwave.
- Thin butter-cream frosting with evaporated milk or warm water. Use only a little liquid and use a icing spatula to mix in.
- Thin cold chocolate butter-cream frosting with a little hot water or hot coffee. Use only a small amount and mix in with a icing spatula.
- Always sprinkle toppings on while the frosting is fresh, wet and sticky.
- When the frosting is too dry for topping to stick, thin it with a little water or milk.
- Store butter-cream frosting in an air tight container in the refrigerator.
- Fresh is best, so don't make butter-cream frosting in advance if possible.

- Always let the butter-cream warm to room temperature before thinning it down for use.

Boiled frosting will not store well. Use what is needed and discard the rest. It's not worth the worry of trying to save. Boiled frosting will last only for a couple of days. Plan for it to be eaten quickly or else use butter-cream frosting.

- When you have a large amount of boiled frosting left over—make snow balls. Peel the paper from cupcakes or use cut cake squares and apply a thick coat of frosting around the cake (use your hands). Roll the cake in loose coconut and place in cupcake liners.

- Colored decorettes, nut-meats and coconut (raw or toasted) makes good topping for both butter-cream and boiled frosting.

> *"Buy emulsified shortening for making cakes and frostings at your local bakery. Ask them about selling you some pre-mixed fondant and boiled frosting base."*

INGREDIENTS FOR FROSTINGS

SUGAR: Powdered sugar used in butter-cream frosting must be lump free. Powdered sugar should always be sifted. Granulated sugar used in boiled frosting must be clean and can not contain any bits of shortening, oil, or butter.

SHORTENING: Emulsified shortening, margarine, or butter may be used in butter-cream frosting. Use an emulsified shortening if you want a pure white frosting. (Ask your local baker to sell you some emulsified shortening.) Use margarine or butter if you like the flavor (the frosting will have a pale yellow color). Butter is an excellent ingredient to use in a chocolate flavored butter-cream frosting.

MILK: Use milk in a butter-cream frosting to enhance the flavor. Milk may also be used to thin heavy frosting to a spreadable consistency.

WATER: Use warm or cold water in butter-cream frosting. Sometimes warm water will cause shortening; especially butter or margarine to separate. Add water slowly.

CREAM: Heavy cream is delicious in butter-cream frosting. Cream must be fresh because it imparts a flavor and color. Cream will also cause the frosting to break down quicker than milk or water. Cream is very good in chocolate butter-cream frosting.

EGG WHITES: Use only fresh, clean egg whites

in boiled frosting If using cold egg whites make sure they come to room temperature.

COCOA: Use fresh, lump free cocoa in butter-cream frosting. When the cocoa is lumpy, push through a sifter.

CHOCOLATE: Use fresh unsweetened baking chocolate in butter-cream frostings. Chocolate will absorb odors and flavors. Store chocolate tightly sealed, in a cool, odor free place. Melt unsweetened baking chocolate over a water bath using very low heat, or better yet in a microwave oven. Add the melted chocolate slowly to butter-cream frosting.

FRUIT: Small amounts of crushed, fresh fruit may be substituted for the liquid in butter-cream frosting. Use a flavor of the same type as the fruit. (apricot flavor added with crushed apricots, etc.) Care must be taken that the butter-cream does not separate when crushed fruit is added to the mix.

SALT: Salt enhances the flavor of frostings, but is not needed and very little, if any, should be used.

SPICES: Cinnamon is a good spice to use in butter-cream and fondant frosting. Use just a tiny amount.

COCONUT: Fresh, moist coconut is a very good covering for both butter-cream and boiled frosting. Lightly toasted coconut is also good to sprinkle on freshly iced items.

NUT-MEATS: Chopped nut-meats is a good covering for butter-cream frosting. Sprinkle nut-meats on the frosting while still wet and sticky. Use only nut-meats that have been stored properly. Taste nut-meats before using because they go rancid very quickly when not stored properly.

DIET MARGARINE, LOW CALORIE MARGARINE: These products are not made to be used in frosting. They contain excessive air or water and should not be used as a shortening substitute.

ALMOND PASTE: Almond paste is used in frostings for flavor. It must be mixed lump free before adding any thinning ingredients.

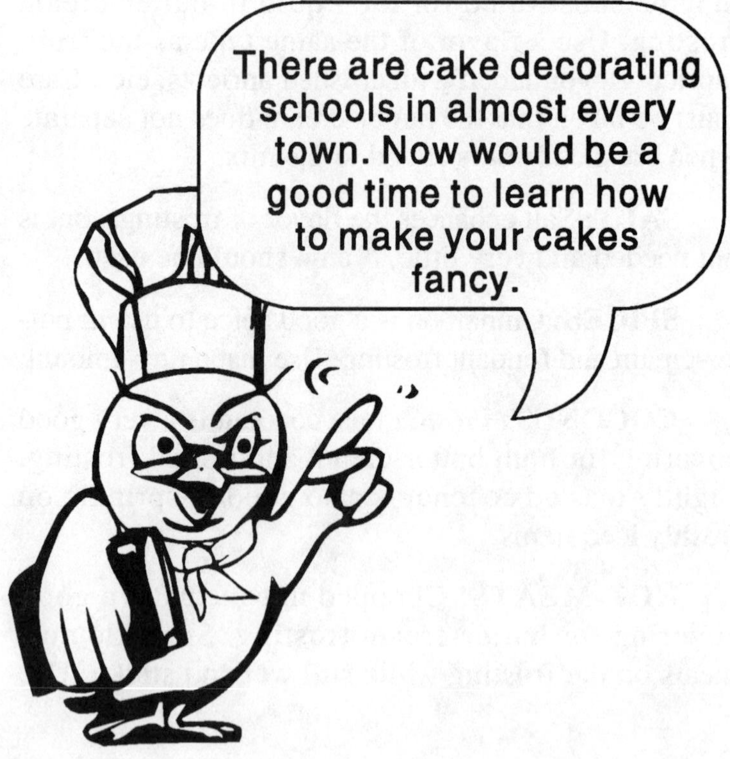

Chapter 3 COOKIES

And

Brownies

Chapter Three——Cookies & Brownies

Contents

CHAPTER THREE 103

CHAPTER THREE

COOKIES

Making cookies is perhaps the easiest of all baking projects. However, since your kitchen is unique and you are unique, you're going to have problems. Read over these trouble-shooting hints before you start baking. Refer to them anytime you have a problem.

Teaching children to make cookies is an excellent way to introduce them to the discipline of using recipes. They will learn the value of doing things correctly and with a purpose. The finished treat is reward enough for doing a good job.

Grandma's sugar cookies were unique because her ingredients were unique to her time. They say our ingredients are better, improved, whatever, but one thing is for sure—they are different. Rather than trying to duplicate Grandma's cookies it's far better to make great cookies by using the ingredients that are available to you today.

Many home bakers make cookies from pre-mixed ingredients which will produce excellent cookies. When using a batter made from a pre-mix, frozen, or ready-to-bake you will find the following methods of preparation, baking tips, finishing tips, and cookie handling tips to be of value.

Using pre-mixed ingredients saves a little time and reduces the needed skill level as far as scaling and mixing goes. However, *all the other parts of cookie handling is exactly the same as making from scratch.* Using these suggestions will save you time and money no matter which form of mixing you choose.

Use a pizza pan or cake pan to bake big cookies, brownies and flat bread. Sometimes things taste better in a different shape.

TIPS

COOKIE MIXING

Mixing cookies has come a long way since the days of a big mixing bowl and a wooden spoon. We have fantastic mixers with a variety of specialized mixing arms. Read the mixer's directions thoroughly and use the mixing arms designed for cookies.

Be very careful that the mixer does not over heat while mixing a heavy cookie dough. If the mixer's motor pulls down or smells hot—stop at once.

Take out some of the dough and add a little liquid. Mix the liquid in then add back the remainder of the dough and enough liquid to thin the dough to its proper consistency.

❖ When the cookie dough is dry, add an egg yolk instead of water. Water makes a dough tough. The fat content of an egg yolk will keep the dough tender.

❖ Cover cookie dough between baking batches. The dough will dry out quickly and become unworkable.

❖ Cookie dough freezes well (6 to 12 months). Wrap tightly and freeze leftovers for next time.

❖ Crumbly cookies may be caused by overmixing the batter. Cream the shortening and sugar together, add liquids and then carefully mix in flour, fruit, chips and nut-meats. Over-mixing the flour will cause crumbly cookies.

Note →

- Care should also be taken to use only cool liquids. Mixing generates heat from bowl friction. Heat may melt the shortening and most certainly will cause the baking powder or baking soda to begin its chemical reaction.

- Dry, hard cookies are caused by over-mixing the batter, over-baking, dry fruit/coconut, too much water or a lack of fat. Excessive salt can also cause cookies to be hard.

Duplication of other people's baking is very difficult. Invariably they do things to the recipe that is not written down. A little extra vanilla, or even a change in mixing time will make a noticeable difference in the finished cookie. Also, their oven will always have different baking characteristics than yours.

First pinpoint the differences between your cookies and theirs. Then make the changes in the recipe to offset the difference. Determine by crust color, taste or texture where theirs is different. Crust color being lighter or darker will usually mean a difference in oven temperature or baking time. Taste difference will signal a need for more or less flavoring or spice. Texture difference can mean either baking time or mixing procedure.

The most important thing to remember about baking anything, is that a recipe should only be used as a guide. Make cookies the way you like.

- ❖ Use the same measuring cups and spoons to measure ingredients. Measuring cups and spoons will differ in the amount they hold. One type is for measuring dry ingredients and the other is for liquids. Usually the difference in volume isn't much, but any difference will effect the correct ingredient balance. Fill a cup with water, then pour that water into another cup. When the level matches, use both cups to measure different liquids. Check measuring spoons in the same way.

COOKIE BAKING

Whether making cookies from scratch or from a pre-mix, correct baking is essential to making great cookies.

- ❖ Turn on the oven about twenty minutes before using. By doing this the temperature will be more accurate when you start baking. Set your oven at 350 degrees.

- ❖ **Note** ➡ When the heat shuts off, check the oven's temperature with an oven thermometer. Place the thermometer at different points (front and back) and at different levels (bottom, middle and top shelf). The results will let you see how to best bake cookies in your unique oven.

- ❖ Use cookie sheets with low sides. Heat will circulate around them evenly and give you a better bake. Also make sure that there is at least 1 to 2 inches of space around the pan. This will let the oven heat evenly.

- ❖ When the recipe reads — bake for ten minutes; set the timer for eight minutes and check the cookies. Each oven is different. A good baking practice is to check on baking progress. Use a spatula and gently lift a cookie to check the bottom.

- ❖ Cookies continue to bake on the hot sheet after they are removed from the oven. Take cookies out a little early rather than when they are completely done. Establish a minimum and maximum baking time for each type of cookie.

Note

- Cookies baking too fast on the bottom is usually caused by excessive bottom heat in the oven. Try putting one shelf at the lowest position and cover the shelf with a sheet of aluminium foil or an empty baking sheet. Put the cookie sheet on a shelf half way up in the oven. This will cause the heat to flow more evenly around the cookies and not over-bake their bottoms.
- New pans or those coated with a dark release agent will cause cookies to over-bake on their bottoms. Double stack, (place one pan inside another) to end this pesky problem.
- Always season new pans (before using) by applying a thin coat of vegetable oil and placing them in a 400 degree oven for about twenty minutes. Wipe out the oil, cool and then prepare the pans as usual for baking.
- Cookies stick to the baking sheet when the sheet is not properly prepared for baking. Be sure that the sheet is seasoned before using, if new. Do not use detergents for cleaning. Wipe the sheet clean with a lightly greased cloth then wipe with a dry cloth or paper towel.

- Cool the sheet completely between batches. Putting cookie dough on a hot or warm baking sheet will sometimes cause them to stick.
- Remove cookies from the baking sheet

while they are still warm. Use a spatula when necessary and place them on a wire rack to cool completely.

- ❖ Using parchment paper will prevent cookies from sticking and keep cookie sheets clean.

- ❖ **Note** → If you like soft centered cookies, chill the cookies after placing on the baking sheet. Bake them at a higher temperature than called for, but watch closely. Remove the cookies from the oven when they are light brown.

- ❖ When cutting or bagging cookies; try to make them all the same size. They'll bake evenly that way.

- ❖ Most cookies should bake in ten to twelve minutes. Start with an oven temperature of 350 degrees and go up five degrees until the cookies are baked ten or twelve minutes. Longer baking times will cause the cookies to be dry.

- ❖ Do not overcrowd the cookies on their baking sheet. Let the hot air circulate around each cookie.

COOKIE FINISHING AND STORING

Finishing cookies may be the most important part of making them. Eye appeal always heightens taste appeal. Make them pretty!

- ❖ Make cookies shine by mixing a pinch of salt with a fresh egg. Beat the egg and salt together (only a little), then let the mixture sit for about fifteen minutes. Brush the egg mixture on each cookie before baking.
- ❖ Sprinkle on a little granulated sugar when desired (before baking). Egg wash is a great topping on Short Bread cookies.
- ❖ Lightly toast coconut or oatmeal for use as a topping after the cookie is baked. Brush the cookie with egg white to make the coconut stick.
- ❖ Melt chocolate (thin with a few drops of vegetable oil) and dip half the cookie. Place the cookie on wax paper and chill only until the chocolate sets up. Serve at room temperature.
- ❖ Cookies freeze well and also will stay fresh when they are sealed in an airtight container.

- ❖ Never mix types of cookies when storing or packing for gifts. Baking soda picks up odors and so does chocolate. When different types of cookies are placed together they all will pick up the dominate odor. Ginger cookies will make all the other cookie types taste like ginger and so on.

Sending cookies through the mail makes for a great surprise, but you should always plan on about seven days in transit. Send cookies like Sugar Cookies, Ginger Snaps and Short Bread. Seal them air-tight and in separate bags. Experiment by sealing and letting your cookies sit for at least five days. If they are still good and are not crumbly, they will probably ship fine.

❖ Popped popcorn is a good packing material to pack around the bags of cookies as you place them in the shipping box.

❖ For holidays or parties, color granulated sugar with a bit of food coloring and sprinkle on un-baked sugar cookies. Lightly press the cookies flat with the bottom of a drinking glass and bake as usual.

❖ Use as little flour as possible when rolling out or cutting cookies. The excess flour will draw moisture from the cookie and also ruin their finished appearance.

❖ Use bread type flour (all purpose flour) for dusting the cookie cutting surface. Bread flour will brown quickly and not ruin the cookie's appearance.

Note →

❖ Freshen up frozen or stored pre-baked cookies by placing them in the oven (300 degrees for 5 minutes) or better yet, place in the microwave for a few seconds.

❖ Chocolate chip cookies may have a white haze on the chips and heating in the oven or microwave for a few seconds will make them taste and look like fresh baked.

- Use high quality jam, not jelly to dot or spread on cookies. Jelly is thin, weak in flavor and not suited for cookies. Sandwich peanut butter or raspberry jam between your Vanilla Wafer cookies for a taste sensation.
- Lightly toast macaroon coconut to make a super good topping.
- Use glazed cherries to decorate Butter Wafer cookies or any cookie that needs a splash of color. Place a small piece of the cherry on the top of each cookie before baking.
- Glazed cherries do not have much flavor, so use almond extract in the cookie dough when you want a cherry taste.
- Try toasting coconut, nut-meats and oatmeal before adding to the mix. Toasted coconut will give cookies a new and special flavor. Adding food coloring to coconut will give a festive air to your cookies. Color small amounts of coconut with different liquid food colors, then blend them together before adding to the mix.

A QUICK TOUR OF COOKIE FAULTS

EXTERNAL APPEARANCE

The crust is too dark—Causes

- ☞ Your oven temperature was too high.
- ☞ Too much milk or sugar in the recipe.
- ☞ You did not mix correctly.

The crust is too light—Causes

- ☞ Your oven temperature was too low.
- ☞ Too much liquid in the mix.
- ☞ You did not mix correctly.

Your cookies spread too much—Causes

- ☞ Too much baking soda in the recipe.
- ☞ Your oven was too cool.
- ☞ You used too much shortening.
- ☞ You creamed the mix too long.
- ☞ Too much liquid in the mix.
- ☞ Too much sugar or syrup in the mix.

Does not spread enough—Causes

- ☞ Not enough baking soda in the recipe.
- ☞ Too much baking powder in the recipe.
- ☞ Your oven was too hot.
- ☞ Not enough shortening in the mix.
- ☞ Not enough sugar or syrup in the mix.
- ☞ Not enough creaming of the mix.

- ☞ Not enough liquid in the mix.

INTERNAL APPEARANCE

Dry and Crumbly—Causes

- ☞ Too much baking time.
- ☞ You did not mix correctly.
- ☞ You added too much flour to the mix.
- ☞ Your oven temperature was too high.
- ☞ Too much sugar or syrup in the mix.

Soft and sticky—Causes

- ☞ Not enough baking time.
- ☞ You did not mix correctly.
- ☞ You did not use enough flour in the mix.
- ☞ You put too much sugar or syrup in the mix.
- ☞ Your oven temperature was too low.

Bad flavor—Causes

- ☞ You did not mix correctly.
- ☞ You added too much flavor.
- ☞ You added too much baking soda or baking powder.
- ☞ You did not correctly store your batter or finished cookies.
- ☞ You did not use enough sugar in the mix.

COOKIE HINTS

BAKING

- Bake cookies at 355 to 365 degrees in a regular oven. Bake cookies at 335 to 345 degrees in a convection oven.
- Check the bottom of the cookie for correct browning.

- Cookies continue to bake after removing from the oven. Always remove as browning begins.
- Cool cookies quickly on a cake rack.

MIXING

- Follow the formula mixing procedure exactly. Use cold water. Do not over-mix the batter.
- Measure the baking soda and baking powder exactly. Measure the flavor exactly.
- Use only clean equipment.

HANDLING

- Cool on cake racks and store as soon as possible.
- Store each type of cookie in an air tight

container. Baking soda will pick up odors, so do not store the batter or finished cookies where they may pick up odors.

- ❖ Avoid making the cookie batter until it can be formed and baked. **NOTE:** *Unless you freeze the batter.*

- ❖ Raw cookie batter will not keep well unless it is frozen immediately after mixing. Baking soda and baking powder begin their actions almost immediately if the batter is warm. Therefore, (*if you want cookies to be the best they can be*) keep the batter as cool as possible and freeze it if you plan on making cookies at a later date.

USING YOUR MICROWAVE

Baking cookies in microwave oven is not usually the best way to do it. Crust color, texture and spread will be different than cookies baked in a conventional oven. It is best to bake in a conventional oven and use the microwave to freshen up cookies. The next time you bake cookies try to bake a few in the microwave. If the results are what you expect them to be, then it's OK to bake that particular cookie in a microwave.

- Chill cookie dough before baking in the microwave.
- Bake in the microwave on full power. The following times are only guides. Your microwave may be faster or slower.
- 3 cookies———1 minute on full power.

  6 cookies———1 1/2 to 1 3/4 minutes on full power.

  9 cookies———2 to 2 1/2 minutes on full power.
- Chill cookie dough and form into 1 inch balls then flatten with the bottom of a drinking glass or use the palm of your hand.
- Form chilled cookie dough into rolls (about 2 inches in diameter) and slice off cookies about 1/4 to 1/2 inch thick. The thicker cookies will almost always be very soft in the center after baking.

- Place the cookies on waxed paper for baking in the microwave.
- Let the cookies cool completely before removing from the waxed paper.
- Defrost baked cookies for only a few seconds on SIMMER. Place the cookies on a paper plate and cover with a paper towel for defrosting.
- Freshen up and heat cookies on SIMMER. Use only a few at a time and give them only about 30 seconds. (*Many microwaves are different in the power they have, so use these times only as guides.*)

Use your microwave to thaw frozen cookie dough.
Always use the low power setting.

TIPS

SOLUTIONS

QUESTION: *How can I make Oatmeal cookies better tasting?*

Add a small amount of cinnamon. Chopped raisins, dates or nut-meats will make oatmeal cookies taste great.

QUESTION: *Why do my Ginger cookies taste flat?*

Add a very small amount of ground clove to the mix. Clove will give ginger cookies zest, but don't over do it.

QUESTION: *Why do my Chocolate chip cookies taste great when they are fresh baked, but the next day their flavor is gone?*

Warm cookies always taste better than cold ones. Heat releases the flavor of chocolate and nutmeats. Try warming cookies in the microwave oven for a few seconds or in a 300 degree oven for about 5 minutes.

QUESTION: *Why do my sugar cookies get very hard the next day after they are baked? They also taste flat.*

Use cake type flour in the mix and do not press them thin when mashing them out. Press them half way down with your fingers, then sprinkle on a little granulated sugar and finish pressing to a little over one-forth inch thick with the bottom of a drinking glass. Thin sugar cookies will always bake crisp. Experiment with different thickness until you are satisfied, then make all the sugar cookies that thick. No matter what the recipe reads, you should always make sugar cookies the way you like. Do not over-mix or over-bake sugar cookies. Sugar cookies will be very light brown on their bottoms when they are done. If their tops are brown — they are over-baked and will be hard. Double the vanilla extract called for in the recipe when you want to punch up their flavor.

QUESTION: *What's the best way to store baked cookies?*

Wrap cookies tightly, then freeze. They should keep in the freezer for 6 to 12 months. Thaw in their package to room temperature. Heat in a 300 degree oven for 5 minutes or for a few seconds in your microwave. Cookie dough freezes well (6 to 12 months, when it's wrapped correctly) and the dough takes up less space than baked cookies. Thaw in its package to room temperature, then bake as usual. Bake half a batch and freeze the other half until next time.

QUESTION: *Is it all right to store or freeze different types of cookies together?*

No. They will absorb each others odors and characteristics. Crispy cookies will get soft and soft cookies will dry out. Store or freeze each type of cookie separate from any other.

QUESTION: *Can I safely store my cookies uncovered in the refrigerator?*

No. They will absorb odors and moisture.

QUESTION: *Can I use fresh fruit in making cookies?*

Using fresh fruit in cookies is difficult. The best way would be to process the fruit into a thick sauce. Substitute the sauce for any water you put in the mix. Example: Fresh apple sauce is much better to use than finely chopped fresh apples.

QUESTION: *I've stored my nut-meats in the refrigerator and they have an off flavor. Is there anything I can do to save them?*

No. The oil in nut-meats goes rancid rather quickly and can't be saved once it has gone bad. Nut-meats will also pick up odors that will affect their taste. Seal tightly for storage and use them as quickly as possible. Freezing nut-meats will protect them longer than storing in the refrigerator, but it's best to use them quickly.

QUESTION: *I got a little water in my chocolate while it was melting. Now my chocolate is full of lumps, must I throw it away?*

No. Stir in one teaspoon of vegetable oil for each ounce of chocolate.

This trick may save the chocolate when there is not a lot of moisture in it. Be very careful and avoid getting any moisture in the melting chocolate.

QUESTION: *I tried to melt chocolate morsels in my microwave and they won't melt. I have a lumpy mess. What can I do?*

Some brands of chocolate morsels are not pure chocolate. They won't melt well. Sometime the chocolate morsels are dried out, old or have gathered moisture from being stored in your refrigerator. They won't melt well. Pure chocolate morsels (that are fresh) should melt well in the microwave. Try adding a teaspoon of oil for each ounce of chocolate. Adding oil may work, but since chocolate morsels can vary somewhat in composition, it may not work. Read the label and buy only pure chocolate morsels.

QUESTION: *I don't like the mess and we don't have the time to mix cookies from scratch. However, I love their fresh baked taste, so I buy pre-mixed cookie dough. Do I need to study your book?*

Yes. Probably more cookies are ruined by improper baking than anything else. Correct handling of the dough before baking, placement in the oven and the number of cookies on each pan are important factors in making perfect cookies. Also, when you plan to store any baked cookies or cookie dough, our suggestions may be helpful.

TIPS ON COOKIES

CHOCOLATE CHIP COOKIES

Chocolate chip cookies are probably the most popular of all cookies. Here are some tips to make them your favorite.

- Always add the chocolate morsels last to the mix. It's best when they are very cold. Just barely stir the morsels in—don't over-mix.
- Cream the shortening and sugar well. All the rest of the ingredients can be just mixed in, but proper creaming of the shortening and sugar is important.
- Make sure that the baking pans are cool between cookie batches.
- Substitute cherry flavored morsels for 1/2 of the chocolate morsels for a new taste treat.
- **Note** Drop the cookies extra thick (use an ice cream scoop), flatten the top a little, then place the cookie sheet in the refrigerator for twenty minutes. Take the sheet from the refrigerator and bake at 375 degrees until the cookie's edges are slightly brown and you will have a soft centered delight.
- Substitute white chips for the chocolate chips and make extra sweet cookies.

SUGAR COOKIES, LEMON SUGAR COOKIES

Sugar cookies are really an old fashion treat that is never out of style.

- ❖ Bake sugar cookies until they are barely brown around the edges. They will finish baking after they are removed from the oven.
- ❖ **Note** → Cream the sugar and shortening thoroughly. All the rest of the ingredients should be just mixed in, but good creaming of the sugar and shortening is very important.
- ❖ Add lemon zest and substitute a little lemon juice for part of the water, plus a few drops of yellow food color will give an excellent lemon sugar cookie.

PEANUT BUTTER COOKIES

- ❖ Always add peanut butter as the last ingredient to the recipe. It's very easy to overmix peanut butter cookies and the cookies will be greasy if you do.
- ❖ Mix in the peanut butter only until it is blended.
- ❖ **Note** → Bake the proper length of time. A little under-bake is much better than to overbake peanut butter cookies.
- ❖ Use crunchy peanut butter instead of

smooth when you want more peanut flavor.

- Use plenty of vanilla extract. Vanilla will bring out the peanut butter taste.

OATMEAL COOKIES, OATMEAL—RAISIN COOKIES

- Add raisins with the sugar and mix dry until the raisins are crushed. Add shortening to the mix and cream well together.
- Add a little cinnamon to bring out the flavor of the oatmeal and the raisins.

- Use Old Fashion Oatmeal (Three Minute, is okay) in oatmeal cookies. Instant oatmeal will dissolve and make a heavy cookie.
- Chopped nut-meats and finely chopped fresh apple is a good addition to oatmeal cookies.
- Be careful not over-bake oatmeal cookies. Less is better. Remember, cookies continue baking after they are removed from the oven.

GINGER SNAP COOKIES

- Use only fresh ground ginger spice. Ginger loses flavor with age and should be replaced when you've had it a long time.

- Bake ginger snaps — well done. When they are under-baked they will be soft, but maybe that's OK. They are still delicious.

CHOCOLATE COOKIES

- Be careful about over-baking chocolate cookies. Since they are already brown, it's hard to tell when they are done. Time the first batch and then add or take away from that time.

Note →

- Add a little *dustless* black pepper to your chocolate cookies. Sounds odd, but black pepper makes for a new taste twist.
- Use Dutch Process Cocoa instead of regular cocoa in chocolate cookies for a new look and taste.

VANILLA WAFER COOKIES

- Bag out vanilla wafer cookies as soon as you have finished mixing them. This batter will not tolerate sitting around.
- Vanilla wafer cookies must have a good bake. They should be medium brown all over.
- When vanilla wafer cookies are over-baked, they will be hard and crispy, but when they are under-baked they will not be good at all.

COOKIE INGREDIENTS

A cup of sugar, two of flour, a stick of butter, a couple of eggs, a dash of salt, a teaspoon of baking soda, a little vanilla—Ingredients to make cookies sound simple enough. But are they?

Once upon a time, sugar was simply sugar, flour was simply flour, and butter was only butter. Eggs are still eggs, but almost everything else has changed—ingredients have gotten better.

We have a choice of sugars, flours and shortening. Ingredients are now specialized to suit our baking needs. Granulated sugar, comes in regular grind, fine grind and extra fine grind. We can get all-purpose flour, cake flour, bread flour and several specialized types of flour. Instead of butter we may choose a flavored margarine with no cholesterol or an excellent all-purpose shortening.

Your chance for successful baking has never been better. Your opportunity to create a personal baking masterpiece is almost assured.

A pre-mix package of cookie dough, whether in a bag, box, or frozen in a tube is a mixture of ingredients. Granted, these pre-mixes are great time savers, but they still demand careful preparation in order to be special.

Listed are several tips about ingredients for baking cookies and a little information which is just nice to know.

BAKING POWDER: Baking powder and baking soda will lose its kick with age. Seal it tightly after use to keep out moisture and odors.

BAKING SODA: Baking soda causes cookies to spread when baked. Baking powder causes cookies to rise and be crunchy.

SUGAR: Cookies are best when a fine-grind granulated sugar is used. Coarse sugar causes cookies to spread excessively and crumble. Powdered sugar causes cookies to be tight-grained and dry. Brown sugar should be moist and lump free. Usually the lumps in brown sugar are very hard and must be pressed through a sieve to remove them.

FLOUR: All-purpose and pastry flour is fine for most cookies. A mixture of one third cake flour to two thirds all-purpose flour is better. Use straight cake flour in sugar cookies.

SHORTENING: All-purpose shortening or hydrogenated shortening will make almost any cookie. A mixture of three-fourths all-purpose shortening and one-fourth real butter is better tasting. The butter should be cool, but not hard, when blending with the shortening.

EGGS: Eggs should always be fresh. The egg's size is very important. When the recipe doesn't say—use large eggs.

SALT: Use very little salt and add at the end of mixing, before the flour is completely mixed in. Salt causes the flour to toughen and can make cookies hard.

COLORING: Never use excessive food coloring. Some food coloring has a taste and may give cookies an off flavor.

WATER: Use very cold water in making cookies (unless the recipe reads differently). Cold water will help keep the mix from separating. Cold fruit juice is a great substitute for water if you like the fruit flavor.

BROWN SUGAR: Brown sugar frequently gets dry and lumpy. Lumpy brown sugar can be brought back to life by adding a little cold water and either sifted or placed in a blender.

FRUIT: Dried fruit (such as raisins) should be soaked in a bowl of hot water for about ten minutes. This will plump them a little, but will not make them too tender.

NUTS: Nut-meats should always be sampled before using. The oil they contain goes rancid rather quickly and can ruin the taste of your cookies. Nut-meats freeze well and should be stored in the freezer, not in the refrigerator. Nut-meats will absorb odors.

COCONUT: Freshen up coconut by adding a little hot water and tumbling until the water is absorbed.

CHOCOLATE: If you've stored chocolate morsels in the refrigerator and they are covered with a white haze, don't worry, that's normal. However, chocolate will absorb odors and should always be sealed tightly and stored at a cool temperature. Also, chocolate will haze over when allowed to heat over 100 degrees while melting. Melt chocolate in the microwave when possible. If you must melt it on the stove, use very low heat. Put the chocolate in a bowl, then place the bowl in a pan containing water. Avoid getting water in the melting chocolate. Water will cause chocolate to lump. When the melted chocolate is very thick, add a small amount of vegetable oil or cocoa butter to thin it down. *Never add water to thin melted chocolate.*

COCOA: If you like chocolate cookies more flavorful, add a little more cocoa to the mix. Cocoa will dry the batter out, so you must add a little more shortening or an extra egg yolk. Make a thick paste out of cocoa and vegetable oil for use in cookie mixes and icing toppings.

SPICE: Use fresh spices in cookies. Spice loses flavor with age and can sometimes taste like something else altogether. Remember, a little spice goes a long way.

VANILLA EXTRACT: Use plenty of vanilla extract. Extracts are alcohol based and much of the flavor may bake out in the oven.

ALMOND EXTRACT: Use almond extract along with vanilla extract to make cherry cookies taste like cherries.

ORANGE EXTRACT: A little orange extract added to a chocolate cookie gives it a special flavor. Don't be afraid to experiment with flavors. Always use a little and build the flavor up.

BROWNIES

Brownies are easy to make from scratch and are available in a world of pre-mix packages. Almost all the pre-mixes will make a good brownie, but scratch brownies can be customized to your favorite taste. Brownies are perhaps the most forgiving of all treats. Brownies are usually good even when they are not quite right.

Mixing technique (whether from scratch or a mix) is the most critical stage in making good brownies. Careful baking time is the other.

Making brownies is a good practice for beginning bakers because even mistakes can sometimes be saved. Brownies are more complicated than cookies, but not as complicated as cake making. Cookie baking requires very little discipline in using correct technique. Brownie baking, however, requires just enough discipline to make an excellent second learning step for those interested in becoming good home bakers.

Any type mixer will do fine for mixing brownies. Use the beaters designed for cake mixing. Any baking pan (metal or glass) is all right for baking brownies. Using a spoon and bowl is all right too.

Using pre-mixed ingredients saves a little time and reduces the needed skill level as far as weighing and mixing goes. However, all the other parts of brownie handling is exactly the same as making from scratch. The following tips will save you time, no matter which form of mixing you choose.

MIXING BROWNIES

- Make sure that all the mixing utensils are clean.
- Follow the directions on the box of a premix exactly. Especially notice when the directions call for hot water to be used. When using hot water, the brownies must go into the oven at once after mixing. When cold water is used, you do not have to bake at once.
- When mixing from scratch, follow the recipe exactly and if the recipe calls for hot water, place the brownies in the oven immediately after mixing.
- **Note** → Most recipes call for the baking powder to be added last. Baking powder reacts to heat. Therefore, it is very important to make sure the mix is cool (unless it calls for hot water).
- Do not over-mix brownies. Cream the sugar with the shortening, but mix everything else only enough to blend in. Sometimes the difference between a chewy and a cake type brownie will only be the mixing time. The less you mix, the more soft and chewy the brownie will be. The more air mixed in the batter will cause the texture to be like cake.

BAKING BROWNIES

- Pre-set the oven about twenty minutes before baking. When the oven reaches the pre-set temperature, use an oven thermometer and make sure the setting is correct.
- Season all new baking pans by applying a very thin coat of vegetable oil and baking them empty for about 25 minutes at 400 degrees. Cool completely, wipe dry, LIGHTLY grease them with all-purpose shortening and dust with flour before using.
- When using a spray release agent on pans, make sure that for brownies the spray DOES contain flour. When using a spray release agent that does not contain flour, lightly dust the pan with flour after spraying.
- Note → Heavy steel or glass pans are best for baking brownies. Light weight pans may pop up in the middle (during the bake) and cause the brownie to split open or have excess bottom heat. Light weight baking pans may also cause brownies to burn or be very hard at their edges.
- Most ovens have a tendency to have hot spots. Avoid placing brownies too near the back or side of the oven. In the center of the middle shelf is best.
- Follow the baking time guide in the recipe very closely. On chewy type brownies

wait until the top rises then as soon as the top falls, remove the brownies from the oven. On cake type brownies wait until the center feels firm to the touch before removing the brownies from the oven.

- Your baking environment may cause the brownies to bake several minutes longer than the recipe directions read. Use sight, touch and common sense to determine when they are done.

When the weather keeps you inside—it's a great time to dig out your favorite recipe and make something special.

This is the perfect time to use that box of cake mix or make a fluffy pie. Home baked breads and rolls always make a meal better and warm cookies are the perfect way to say "welcome home".

Get everyone involved and make your home baking a fun project. It's a great way to teach new skills and have fun at the same time.

BROWNIE FINISHING AND STORING

- Brownies are a super treat when they are served without a topping. However, a rich chocolate fondant type frosting will really make them special. Apply a thin layer of frosting while the brownies are warm (not hot). The chocolate frosting will melt slightly and cause a shiny top.
- Apply butter cream frosting when the brownies are cold and use plenty to make thick swirls and designs.
- Note → Add food color to white fondant frosting and use it to make colorful holiday brownies.
- Sprinkle warm frosting with nut-meats, chocolate chips or colored decorettes to give brownies an added touch of goodness.
- Brownies freeze well. Wrap and seal them air tight.

SOLUTIONS

QUESTION: *Why are my brownies always hard and dark?*

Over-baking is usually the reason brownies are hard. Remove chewy type brownies from the oven as soon as they rise and then fall. If you continue to bake them, they will be hard. When the recipe or directions call for hot water in the mix and you use cold water, the brownies will be hard. When you delay in baking the brownies after they are mixed, they may bake out hard. Follow mixing and baking directions closely.

QUESTION: *Why do my brownies have an off flavor?*

The nut-meats you used could be rancid. The baking soda may be old or maybe the cocoa has absorbed odors. Any of these things may cause your brownies to have an off flavor. Make sure that all the ingredients you use are fresh.

QUESTION: *Why are my brownies hard, and have a tough crust around the edges?*

Sometimes the natural result from the recipe will yield a brownie with a tough outer crust. Or it may be the type of pan you use. Trim this crust off and serve it like a cookie. Never judge your brownies doneness by their outer crust. Watch the middle. The chewy type will rise, then fall. The cake type will rise and be firm to the touch.

QUESTION: *Should I try to send brownies through the mail?*

Yes. Brownies are one of the best baked items to mail. Pack them in air tight bags or containers. They should be good for several days. Anytime you mail baked goods, use the fastest method of mailing.

QUESTION: *What is the best way to freeze brownies?*

Wrap them in small packages (as many as you will use at one time). Make sure the packages are air tight and the proper type for freezing.

TIPS ON BROWNIES

PRE-MIXED BROWNIES

Brownie boxed and frozen pre-mixes are usually great tasting. However, they can easily be customized to make them better. It's fun to try new things, so don't be afraid to add a little of this or that.

- ❖ Add extra egg yolk or a little vegetable oil to make brownies moist.
- ❖ Add a little vanilla extract for more flavor.
- ❖ Add some butterscotch or chocolate morsels to really punch up the flavor.
- ❖ Add fresh nut-meats to plain brownies for crunchy goodness.
- ❖ Add a little honey or corn syrup for a better flavor.

SCRATCH BROWNIES

- ❖ Follow the tips given for pre-mix brownies. Just add the extras to the recipe.
- ❖ Substitute peanut butter for about one forth of the shortening in the brownie recipe. Frost these brownies with a butter cream frosting or a chocolate fudge frosting, but

substitute peanut butter for one third of the shortening in the frosting recipe.

- ❖ Melt caramel candy squares and sandwich the melted candy between two layers of brownie batter. Bake as usual. You can, of course, do this tip with a pre-mix batter.
- ❖ Mix brownie batter for a couple of extra minutes when you want more of a cake type brownie.

INGREDIENTS FOR BROWNIES

SUGAR: Fine granulated sugar or granulated sugar is best to use in brownies.

SHORTENING: All-purpose shortening or hydrogenated shortening is best to use in all types of brownies.

FLOUR: Cake type flour or all-purpose flour can be used when making brownies. Do not use bread type flour.

HONEY: Honey can be used to keep the brownies moist and add a little flavor.

CORN SYRUP: Corn syrup can be used instead of honey. Corn syrup will keep the brownies moist.

WATER: Some recipes call for hot water to be added to the brownie mix. When the recipe doesn't mention hot or cold—use cold water.

EGGS: Fresh egg yolks (without the egg white) are best to use in brownies. Some recipes may call for whole fresh eggs and some additional egg yolk. Make sure that the eggs are FRESH. The egg's size is very important. When the recipe doesn't say—use large eggs.

MILK: Powdered milk, fresh milk or evaporated milk mixed 50/50 with water is good to use in brownies.

NUT-MEATS: Many brownie recipes call for nut-meats. Make sure that the nut-meats are fresh and not rancid. Nothing will hide the flavor of rancid nut-meats.

BAKING SODA: Make sure that the baking soda is fresh. An open box of baking soda will pick up odors and flavors, which will ruin the taste of brownies.

BAKING POWDER: Make sure that the baking powder is fresh. When your baking powder has been opened for several months—use from a new can.

CINNAMON: Ground cinnamon is a very good spice to use in brownies. Use only a little.

SALT: Salt is an important flavor ingredient for brownies, but use salt in small amounts.

VANILLA: Vanilla is the primary flavor extract, use plenty. A small amount of orange extract will give a surprising new taste to brownies.

COCOA: Cocoa must be fresh and always tightly re-sealed in the container. Cocoa will absorb odors and have an unpleasant taste when left open or poorly sealed. When cocoa is lumpy, just press through your sifter. A paste of cocoa mixed with melted butter, margarine or oil is a very good way to add cocoa to your brownie mix.

Your Notes

Fresh baked muffins or cookies are perfect to pack in a sack lunch. Add a small can of fruit to make it even better.

Chapter 4

MUFFINS And Quick Breads

Contents

CHAPTER FOUR 147

CHAPTER FOUR

MUFFINS

Making muffins from scratch is easy and can be customized to suit any taste.

Muffin pre-mixes are good, but most are rather bland in flavor. Pre-mixes take almost as much time to prepare as from scratch and never seem to taste as good. Adding fresh fruit or nuts will make it better.

Any mixer will mix muffin batter, just be careful that the batter is not over-mixed. Regular cupcake pans with or without paper will do for baking muffins, however, you may want to buy large pans that are made especially for muffins.

When using a batter made from a pre-mix or frozen you will find these methods of preparation, baking tips, finishing tips, and muffin handling tips to be of value.

Using pre-mixed ingredients saves a little time and reduces the needed skill level as far as weighing and mixing goes. However, all the other parts of muffin handling is exactly the same as making from scratch. Using these suggestions will save you time and money no matter which form of mixing you choose.

We always try to think of new ingredients to add to the muffin batter and put on top for decoration.

This is one time the children can be creative. Let them decide what new muffins you'll make. It's best to show them the ingredient options and they'll pick their favorite. You can make baking fun for everyone by using your imagination and then teaching the kids to use theirs.

Try adding one or more of these to your batter.

- ☺ Chopped nuts of all kinds
- ☺ Crushed pineapple
- ☺ Ground carrots
- ☺ Oat Meal
- ☺ Raisins
- ☺ Chocolate chips
- ☺ Candy coated chocolate
- ☺ Chopped apples
- ☺ All kinds of fruit juice (instead of water)
- ☺ Mashed bananas
- ☺ Chopped dried fruit

Being creative is the best part of home baking. And the best part of being creative with your baking projects is that it is easy to do. Don't be afraid to try something new. It may not be perfect every time, but usually everything you bake will be enjoyed. We try new recipes all the time. Some are average and some are super good. You'll never know what you are missing unless you try new recipes.

"Today would be perfect to make a batch of home baked muffins. Let everyone help and they will taste that much better."

MIXING MUFFINS

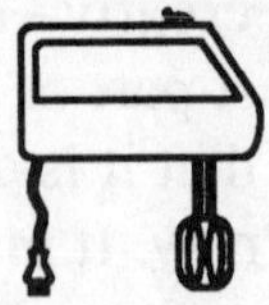

- Use the beaters designed for batter on the mixer. The same ones you use to mix cake batter are fine.

- Make sure that all the utensils are clean. Check the measuring cups and spoons (if you are using more than one set) to make sure that they hold the same volume. Measuring cups and spoons will hold different volumes, some are for dry ingredients and others for liquids.

- Follow mixing times and methods of ingredient addition to the letter. Most failures come from using shortcuts.

- Keep the batter as cool as possible. Keeping the batter cool will let the baking soda and/or baking powder begin action in the oven, where it's supposed to.

- Add frozen blueberries without thawing them. Other frozen fruit should be thawed and chopped into small pieces.

- Fill muffin cups and bake as soon as possible after mixing. It is very important that the muffin batter is kept cool.

- When you can't bake at once, place the batter in the refrigerator until it can be used. Do not try to save the batter for an extended time (overnight).

BAKING MUFFINS

- Pre-set the oven about twenty minutes before baking. When the oven reaches the pre-set temperature, use an oven thermometer to make sure the setting is correct.

- Season all new baking pans by applying a very thin coat of vegetable oil and baking empty for about 25 minutes at 400 degrees. Cool completely, wipe dry and LIGHTLY grease with all-purpose shortening before using.

- For releasing muffins (without papers), the release spray must be one that DOES contain flour. A very thin coating of all-purpose shortening will cause muffins to release. Apply the shortening to muffin pans, but also dust the cups with a thin coating of bread type flour for good release.

- Heavy steel pans are best for baking muffins. Light weight pans may cause the crust to brown before the middle is done.

- Most ovens have a tendency to have hot spots. Always place the muffin pan in the middle of the center shelf. Muffins need a 375 to 385 degree temperature to bake properly. Make sure the oven temperature setting is correct.

- Test for doneness by touching the center of the muffin. The center should feel firm to the touch and spring back to a soft push.

FINISHING AND STORING MUFFINS

Note ❖ Before baking, sprinkle granulated sugar, or brown sugar on top of muffins. Sprinkle around the edges only, leave the middle clean.

❖ Before baking, sprinkle chopped nut-meats on the tops of fruit filled muffins to give them a little extra.

❖ Store extra muffins in the freezer. Muffins freeze well and freezing is the best way to save them.

❖ Wrap muffins in foil for freezing.

❖ Place pre-baked, frozen muffins, unwrapped, in a 350 degree oven for about 15 minutes to heat.

Note ❖ Many types of muffins ship well. Cool them thoroughly and place in plastic bags. Pack with plenty of popcorn (plastic or real) around them.

❖ Place {wrapped in a dry paper towel} in the microwave and heat on high for about 20 to 30 seconds.

SOLUTIONS

QUESTION: *How do I keep muffins from molding?*

Use clean kitchen utensils, cool completely before storing and you shouldn't have a problem with mold.

QUESTION: *Why are my muffins flat on top and stick to the top of the muffin pan?*

You are filling the muffin cups too full. Fill the cups about two-thirds full for best results. You may have excess liquid or baking soda in the mix. Drain excess juice from fresh fruit. Measure baking soda carefully. Grease the top of the muffin pan.

QUESTION: *Why are my muffins sometimes gummy on the top?*

You are not baking them long enough. Don't just bake muffins the amount of time recommended by the recipe. Always test them for doneness. Baking time is variable with the temperature of the muffin batter.

QUESTION: *Why are my muffins heavy and crumbly?*

The batter has probably gotten too warm and the baking soda is ruined.

When the oven's temperature is too cool the muffins will be crumbly. Make sure the batter is kept cool and the oven is set at the proper temperature for baking muffins.

QUESTION: *Why does my muffin batter taste salty?*

Salt keeps the muffins from tasting flat. When you measure carefully and they still taste salty, it is probably that the margarine you use contains a high percentage of salt. Use butter, all-purpose shortening, or change to a different kind of margarine.

TIPS ON MUFFINS

BLUEBERRY MUFFINS

- Slightly under-bake blueberry muffins. They dry out quickly and should have a light bake.

Note

- Sprinkle granulated sugar in a circle around the edges of each muffin before baking them. Do not let too much sugar get on the muffin's center.
- Do not completely thaw frozen blueberries. Wash off any ice crystals and fold the blueberries into the muffin batter. Bake as usual.

STRAWBERRY MUFFINS

- Crush fresh or frozen strawberries through a strainer. You can use the same recipe as using for blueberry muffins, except do not add any water. The crushed strawberries will provide plenty of liquid.
- A teaspoon of lemon juice will enhance the flavor of strawberry muffins.

- Try making quick bread loaves from your strawberry muffin recipe. Add some chopped nuts or raw sunflower seeds for a new flavor.

- Blend a few chopped peaches or fruit cocktail with the strawberries for a colorful treat. Make this recipe into muffins or quick bread loaves.

- Add a few small chocolate chips to the recipe and watch everyone come back for more.

BRAN MUFFINS

- Substitute oatbran for the usual wheat bran.

- Add a tablespoon or two of molasses for flavor.

- Add a handful of raisins for moisture and nutrition.

- Add chopped nuts or raw sunflower seeds for crunchy goodness.

- Oatmeal glazed with brown sugar (cook together in a sauce pan) is wonderful sprinkled over the tops of bran muffins.

ZUCCHINI MUFFINS

- Squeeze any excess juice from the shredded zucchini and substitute for part of the water. When the recipe doesn't call for water—discard the juice. Add the shredded zucchini as the last ingredient to the mix. Zucchini muffins over-mix easily so it's best to fold the zucchini into the mix by hand.

- ❖ Add a little nutmeg to the zucchini muffin mix for a new taste.
- ❖ Add a small box of lime gelatin to the zucchini mix for a surprising flavor.
- ❖ Walnuts and chopped pecans are excellent additions to any zucchini recipe.

CORN BREAD MUFFINS

Note ➡

- ❖ Place a level teaspoon of all-purpose shortening in each muffin cup and heat until the shortening smokes. Pour corn bread batter onto the hot shortening and immediately bake as usual. The hot shortening will cause a thick, delicious bottom crust to form.
- ❖ Add about 8 ounces of shredded American cheddar cheese to the corn bread batter.
- ❖ When you like hot corn bread muffins, add a couple of finely chopped jalapeno peppers.
- ❖ Frozen whole kernel corn is also great to add into corn bread muffin batter.

PLAIN MUFFINS

- ❖ Sift all the dry ingredients together twice.
- ❖ Add all the liquid at one time and mix until

the flour is just moistened. The batter may look lumpy, but that is OK. Over-mixing will cause the muffins to be tough and have long holes on the inside.

❖ Fill the pans about 2/3 full. Have them well greased so that the muffins will come out easily.

❖ Use fresh eggs and make sure all the ingredients are cool.

❖ Do not over-bake muffins or quick breads. They dry out quickly and a light bake is best.

INGREDIENTS FOR MUFFINS

One of the things we like best about making muffins is that we usually have all the ingredients handy.

We hardly ever use my mixer, because a large bowl and a wooden spoon is perfect for the job. Sometimes we just forget the spoon and use our hands to mix the ingredients. The kids think it's *yucky*, but we think it's a lot of fun and they never fail to eat all the muffins.

Less is best with muffins and quick breads. Less mixing and less baking time will make better muffins.

As with all recipes—use quality ingredients of the same brand names so your results will be the same time after time.

SUGAR: Granulated sugar is best for making muffins.

FLOUR: All-purpose flour is good for making muffins. Bread flour is also good to use. Cake flour is best.

WATER: Use cold water in muffins unless the recipe reads otherwise. Since muffin batter uses baking soda and/or baking powder, it is important that the batter be kept cool.

SALT: Salt is important to flavor enhancement,

but is not necessary and should be used sparingly.

BAKING POWDER: Always use fresh baking powder or make sure that it has been stored properly. Baking powder loses strength with age, so fresh is best. Measure carefully.

BAKING SODA: Always use fresh baking soda or make sure that it has been stored properly. Baking soda absorbs odors and loses strength with age. Fresh is best. Measure carefully.

MILK: Fresh milk and powdered milk is fine to use in all types of muffins. Milk makes muffins taste richer and brown better. Use cream for extra richness.

SHORTENING: All-purpose shortening, hydrogenated shortening is good to use in muffins. Butter, margarine and salad oil also work well. Salad oil will make muffins and quick breads seem more moist when they are cool. Add a little oil to the recipe if it tastes dry.

SPICES: Muffins lend themselves to many spices. You can be creative when using spices to flavor muffins. Add zest to a dry pre-mix muffin with the kind of spice you like. Cinnamon and a little ground clove will enhance the flavor of almost any muffin.

FLAVOR: Perk up dry pre-mix muffins with an extra flavor such as vanilla or almond extract. A cherry muffin will be enhanced if you add vanilla and almond extract. Lemon or orange extract (use only a little) will enhance any fruit type muffin.

CHOCOLATE: Small chocolate morsels are best in muffins. Coat them with flour before adding to the mix.

FRUIT: Frozen blueberries, chopped apples, crushed strawberries and peaches are excellent fruits for muffins. Use any excess juice as part of the recipe's liquid. Use apple juice instead of water in a muffin mix for a new flavor.

NUTS: Always make sure that nut-meats are fresh. They get rancid fast and should be tasted before using.

EGGS: Use only fresh eggs in the muffin mix. Eggs separate better when they are at room temperature. Eggs should always be fresh. The egg's size is very important. When the recipe doesn't say—use large eggs.

DIET MARGARINE, LOW CALORIE MARGARINE: These forms of shortening are not made for baking and should never be substituted for shortening in your muffin mix.

QUICK BREADS

Almost all quick breads are made exactly the same as muffins—they are baked in loaves instead of muffin cups.

QUICK BREAD TIPS

- The dried fruits and nuts used in quick breads are usually left in larger chunks than in muffins.
- The baking temperature for quick breads should be about 10 degrees less than for muffins. Use a toothpick to test for doneness.
- Quick breads are best if they are cut and served the day after baking. Cool them completely then wrap tightly and leave at room temperature overnight.
- Fill the loaf pans 2/3 full for best results.

- If the bread dries out too much during baking you should add a little vegetable oil (two tablespoons per loaf) to the mix the next time.
- Coat the loaf pan with very finely chopped nuts to make your quick bread extra tasty.

MICROWAVE HINTS

- Bake muffins in plastic microwave muffin or cupcake pans. You may also use coffee cups lined with muffin papers or custard cups.
- Fill the containers no more than 1/2 way full to allow for the extra volume you will get from microwave baking.
- Do not cover muffins while baking in the microwave.
- Follow the directions on the box or in the recipe for microwave setting and baking times.
- Frozen muffins and quick breads may be defrosted and heated on MEDIUM. Place on a paper plate or towel and cover with plastic wrap or a paper towel or napkin. Defrost or heat only a few muffins at a time to keep from drying them out.

Your Notes

Home baked items make wonderful gifts. Everyone appreciates the special effort and thoughtfulness. A family baking project makes it fun.

Chapter 5

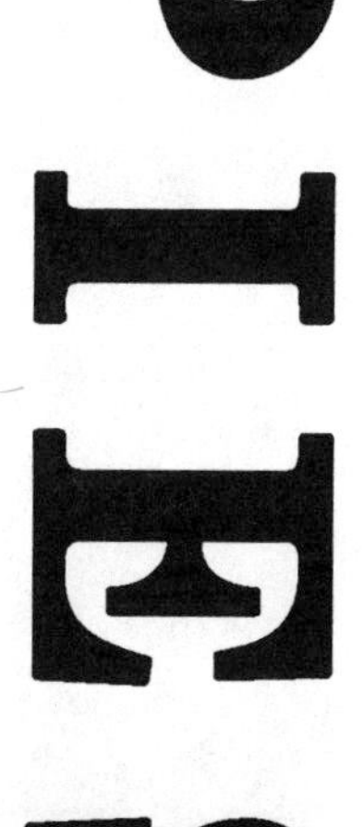

And

Fillings

Contents

CHAPTER FIVE 167

CHAPTER FIVE

PIES & FILLINGS

TWO CRUST PIE: Fruit is the most popular filling for two crust pies. Any kind of fruit mixed with sugar, sometimes spices and a thickener will make a delicious two crust fruit pie. Left-over chicken, pork and beef are also used to make a new and delicious meal when they are baked in small two-crust pies.

DEEP-DISH AND COBBLERS: Deep-dish and Cobblers are pies that are usually baked in a casserole pan. They are thick pies with a crust covering only the top. They are served by the spoonful rather than by the slice. Deep-Dish apple pie in New England is considered a way of life.

ONE CRUST PIE: Single crust pies are used to hold custard type pies such as pumpkin. Cream pies with meringue topping are single crust pies as are refrigerator pies with whipped cream topping.

MIXING PASTRY FOR PIE CRUSTS

The crust of a pie must provide support and often a cover for the pie filling. No matter if the crust is made from scratch or from a pre-mix, it is very important that pie dough pastry be handled gently and not over-mixed.

Pastry is the most popular crust for pies, but graham cracker, crushed cookies and coconut are also used. Pastry crusts are sometimes pre-baked before adding the filling. Graham cracker and crushed cookie types of crusts are usually pre-baked.

- Follow the recipe to the letter when mixing pastry dough. Under-mixed dough will be very flakey and fall to pieces, while over-mixed dough will be mealy and sometimes hard.

- Shortening should be cut into the dough with a fork or tool for mixing pie dough. The shortening lumps should be about pea size to be perfect.

- Very cold water is best to use in mixing pastry dough.

- Use all purpose flour in pastry dough. Bread flour is too tough and cake flour is too soft for making a proper pastry dough.

PASTRY DOUGH

- When using a mixer, make sure that you use the beaters designed for pastry mixing.
- Do not over-mix the dough. When using a food processor, make sure that you do not over-mix the dough. Food procesors mix the dough very quickly.
- Make sure that all utensils are clean.
- Use chilled shortening and ice cold water in the mix. Mix the chilled shortening and dry ingredients (except the salt) together first. These ingredients should be blended well. Water and salt will cause the pastry to be tough, so dissolve the salt in the ice water and add it last. Blend the dough only until the mix is not wet and sticky feeling. Adding the salt/water to the mix last, *with careful blending*, is the key to making tender, flaky pastry.

Note →

GRAHAM CRACKER & CRUSHED COOKIE CRUST

- Mix all the dry ingredients thoroughly when making a graham cracker or crushed cookie crust.
- Add the melted butter or margarine last and blend only until absorbed.

- Do not over-mix. When this type of crust is over-mixed, it will be hard and pasty.
- The crumbs should be wet enough to stick together when squeezed in your hand. If the crumbs do not stick together, mix in a little more melted butter or margarine. Do not get the crumbs too wet, because the crust will taste greasy.
- Pre-bake crumb crusts for four minutes at 350 degrees for best results when you are making refrigerator pies. Cool before filling.

PIE PAN PREPARATION

- Spray pie pans with a release agent before lining them with graham cracker or crushed cookie crusts.
- Use a spray without added flour. A very thin coating of all-purpose shortening rubbed on the pie pan with your fingers will cause the crust to release.
- When a refrigerator type filling is used in a graham cracker crust, it is best to place the pie on a warm surface just long enough to soften the bottom of the crust, causing it to release from the pan.
- **Note** → Glass pans are pretty to look at and extremely useful in making pies, but they are very stubborn about releasing a crumb crust. Wrap a hot towel around the bottom and sides of a pan to warm it enough for easy crust removal.

BAKING PIES

Note

- Turn on the oven about twenty minutes before using. This simple step will help insure the temperature will be more accurate when you start baking.

- Set the oven at 365 degrees. When the heat shuts off, check the oven's temperature with an oven thermometer. Place the thermometer at different points (front and back) and at different levels (bottom, middle, top shelf). The results will let you see how to best bake pies in your unique oven.

- When the recipe reads—"bake for 45 minutes" set the timer for 35 minutes and check the pies. Each oven is different and it's a good baking practice to check on baking progress.

- The most common mistake is to underbake fruit pies, but it's awful to burn the top crust. Top crusts baking too fast are usually caused by excessive top heat in the oven. Cover pies with brown paper or an extra foil pan.

- Whole milk, sprayed or painted, on the pie top will cause it to brown off too fast. Thin the milk-wash with water and it will take longer to brown.

- Pans with a dark colored, non-stick coating will cause pies to bake good on their bottoms.

- ✪ Always season new pans (before using) by applying a thin coat of vegetable oil and placing in a 400 degree oven for about twenty minutes. Wipe the pans clean, cool and prepare as usual for baking. Pans coated with a dark colored, non-stick coating or glass pans do not need seasoning.

FINISHING AND STORING PIES

- Brush the top of a two crust pie with water, milk, evaporated milk, or egg wash—then sprinkle with granulated sugar to make a pretty pie.
- Use a cookie cutter to cut shapes from flat pastry dough and place them on pie tarts and deep-dish pies.
- Wash (with water) and sugar the cut-outs, bake them separately—then place on top of filled tarts, etc..
- Use a spray bottle filled with milk/water to spray wash lattice top fruit pies.

- Cool cream pies completely before placing meringue on them. Hot cream filling may cause the meringue to melt and slide off the pie when it is cut.
- Keep the knife from pulling at the meringue, by dipping the blade in water before cutting.
- Store fruit pies at room temperature. Cover them with foil.

- Fruit pies freeze well. Freeze them raw, don't thaw, just bake as usual (about 45 minutes to 1 hour).
- Freeze pre-baked pies. Wrap in foil. Thaw by placing uncovered in a 350 degree oven until the filling boils (about 20 minutes).

- Store cream and whipped cream pies (covered) in the refrigerator. Meringue breaks down fast, no matter where you store it, so meringue pies must be eaten quickly.
- Whipped cream pies will last longer when wrapped and refrigerated. However, freezing is not recommended.
- **Note** → Brown meringue in a hot oven, about 425 degrees. Browning meringue at lower temperatures may cause the top to form a thick crust.

Wrap or cover all your baked items as soon as they are cool. Freeze left-overs to keep them fresh.

TIPS

A QUICK TOUR OF PIE CRUST FAULTS

EXTERNAL APPEARANCE

If the crust is too light—Causes

- ☞ Not enough milk/sugar in the recipe.
- ☞ Your oven temperature was too low.
- ☞ Your dough was too cold.
- ☞ Your baking time was too short.

If the crust is too dark—Causes

- ☞ Too much milk/sugar in the recipe.
- ☞ Your oven temperature was too high.
- ☞ Your baking time was too long.

INTERNAL APPEARANCE

If the crust is dry and crumbly—Causes

- ☞ Too much milk/sugar in the recipe.
- ☞ You over-baked at a low temperature.
- ☞ Not enough liquid in the recipe.
- ☞ Not enough shortening in the recipe.
- ☞ You used the wrong type of flour.

If the crust is tough—Causes

- ☞ You over-mixed the dough.

- ☞ You used the wrong type of flour.
- ☞ You used too much salt or added too soon in mixing.
- ☞ Your dough was too hot when mixed.
- ☞ You did not use enough shortening in the dough.
- ☞ You used too much water in the dough.

Use the same "Name Brand" ingredients that are in your recipe. Your baking will be much better.

PIE CRUST HINTS

BAKING

- Bake pie crust at 355 to 375 degrees in a standard oven. Bake pie crust at 325 to 355 degrees in a convection oven. Bring the crust to 70 to 80 degrees before baking.
- Wash the crust with a milk wash (evaporated milk) that will give a desired color.
- Note → Bake pies as quickly as possible. Pre-bake shells to a golden brown only. Pre-bake shells to a light brown if more baking is required after filling is added.

MIXING

- Use very cold or ice water. Follow formula method exactly. Use the correct flour (pastry) or all-purpose.
- Do not over-mix the dough.
- Use cool shortening if possible.
- Keep the dough cold during all processing.
- Add the salt with the last addition of water. Salt causes the gluten in flour to toughen.
- All equipment should be clean.

HANDLING

- ✿ Bring (cold) pies to 70 or 80 degrees before baking. Let them cool in a draft free area.
- ✿ Freeze dough which has been properly mixed and handled (always cover).
- ✿ Never let pie dough warm to room temperature before using.
- ✿ Use baked shells as soon as possible.
- ✿ Use raw dough as soon as it matures (usually overnight is best).

SOLUTIONS

QUESTION: *Will chiffon pies freeze satisfactory?*

Yes. Chiffon pies will freeze for up to two weeks. Thaw frozen chiffon pies in the refrigerator.

QUESTION: *Should I refrigerate meringue pies?*

Yes. Meringue pies are usually made with eggs in the filling and any pie with eggs used in the filling should be refrigerated.

QUESTION: *What is a good way to make my pastry crust shine?*

Brush the pastry with a honey and water (50/50) glaze as soon as you remove the pie from the oven. Melt apple or Apricot jelly and brush over the hot pastry for shine and a little flavor.

QUESTION: *Why does my pie crust shrink down from the sides of the pan?*

Pie crust must be not be stretched when putting in the pie pan. Also, besides making it tough, overmixing will cause the crust to shrink away from the sides of the pan.

QUESTION: *Do fruit pies freeze well?*

Yes. Either baked or raw fruit pies may be frozen if they are wrapped correctly.

QUESTION: *Why should I cut the top crust of*

fruit pie before baking?

Cutting the top crust of fruit pies will allow the steam generated while baking to escape. This keeps the pie from breaking at the side and running out of the pan.

QUESTION: *What is the best thickener to use in cream pie fillings?*

What thickener you use (corn starch, flour or eggs) depends upon your taste. Each has its own characteristics and they all work—use the one you like the best.

QUESTION: *Why do my pies stick to the pan after they are cold and I am ready to serve them?*

The shortening in the crust will cause the pie crust to bind itself to the pan when it becomes cold unless you use a release agent on the pan. I always use a hot towel to warm the pie pan before I cut the pie for servings.

QUESTION: *I follow the recipe to the letter, but my filling is always too thick. What can I do?*

You are probably using a different type or brand name of thickening agent from that used by the person who wrote the recipe. It is important to use the same ingredients time after time. If you are not sure what the specific ingredient is—then either cut back on the amount of thickener used or cut back on the cooking time. A recipe is only a guide to follow. It is fine to make changes to suit your unique environment.

QUESTION: *Is it OK to use frozen fruit instead of fresh fruit in my pie filling?*

Yes. However, you must drain off the juice if there is any because it will probably contain a lot of sugar which will change the balance of your recipe. Also it is important to thaw the fruit and drain it before using in the pie.

QUESTION: *Why does my recipe call for lemon juice in the pie filling?*

Lemon juice in a fruit pie filling will restore the tart flavor lost in canning or freezing the fruit. It also acts as a preservative to keep the color and texture the same as when the fruit is added.

QUESTION: *Why is my cream filling full of tiny lumps and runny?*

You have a problem with the way you are adding the eggs. Eggs must be heated by adding a small amount of the hot liquid to them and then "when they are warm" they should be added to the cooking mixture. If you add the eggs cold, they will cook too fast and cause the tiny lumps which prevents them from acting as a thickener. Your filling will be runny and full of lumps.

QUESTION: *I have a problem with keeping my whipping cream the proper consistency. It is either too thick or else it is runny. What can I do?*

Whipping cream is fragile to work with when using it as a pie topping or part of the filling. It must always be as fresh as possible so check the date on it before buying. Mixing time is best done by watching it closely and when you decide it's right—stop the mixer. Add the correct amount of powdered sugar after the cream begins to set up. If you add too much sugar or if you add sugar at the wrong time the cream will be runny. Pay close attention to what you are doing and make notes so that you'll remember how you did it right.

Make sure the cream, bowl, and the beaters have been thoroughly chilled before using. Use a bowl large enough to allow the cream to double in volume. Whip the cream in high speed until it begins to thicken then add about 1/4 cup of powdered sugar to each cup of cream and the flavoring. Continue beating in high speed until the desired volume is reached.

Be sure the filling or fruit is very cool before adding whipped cream to it. Store whipped cream in the refrigerator and use it as soon as possible.

QUESTION: *What is the best kind of chocolate to add to my vanilla cream filling if I want to make a chocolate filling from it?*

Melt semi-sweet chocolate chips and add a little vegetable oil to make a smooth paste before adding to the vanilla cream. This will make a light chocolate filling. Add vegetable oil to cocoa to make a paste then put as much of this paste into the vanilla filling as you want in order to make a dark chocolate filling.

PIE FILLINGS TIPS

FRUIT PIES

- Save the drained juice from frozen or canned fruit and use fruit juice instead of water in the recipe. This is only a good idea if the fruit is packed in water—not syrup.
- Add fresh butter to your fruit pie filling after it has been cooked. Or dot pieces of butter over the fruit before placing on the top crust.

- Don't cut apples pieces too thin when using fresh apples. Larger chunks will hold together and have more apple flavor.
- Use a little red food color and a drop or two of almond extract in cherry pies when using fresh or canned cherries.
- Use a little yellow food color and a teaspoon of lemon juice in apricot and peach fruit pies. The lemon juice will enhance their flavor and also help keep a bright color.
- Use cinnamon and a little ground clove to flavor raisin pie. Let raisins sit in hot water to plump before cooking them in a filling.
- Mix a few raisins with fresh chopped apples and make an easy, new apple pie.

✿ Apply any glaze, for shine, after the fruit pie is baked.

Do not over-cook pie fillings, especially those with corn starch used as the thickener. The filling will break down and quickly become watery. Over cooking fillings made with flour will cause the filling to be thick. Add the thickening mixture as soon as the water/sugar comes to a boil and cook until the mixture becomes clear and thick enough to coat the spoon or whisk.

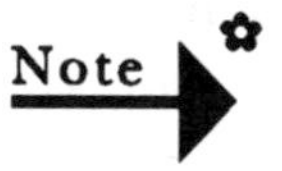

✿ Add canned fruit pie fillings to a pre-baked pie crust and either top with pre-baked pastry cut-outs or whipped cream. When using canned fruit pie fillings, you don't have to bake the pie.

✿ Dried apricots, apples and peaches make excellent fruit pies. Always plump them until soft in boiling water before making into a pie filling.

CREAM PIES

Cook cream pie filling in a double boiler or in a very thick sided pot. Cream fillings scorch easily when cooked over direct heat. A copper pot is best. It is very important to clean a copper pot each time you use it. Use an equal mixture of vinegar and salt to clean the copper.

✿ Melted chocolate morsels or baking chocolate added to your favorite vanilla cream filling will make a good chocolate pie filling.

- Stir a little canned fruit pie filling into your vanilla cream filling to make a delicious fruit cream pie.
- Dip sliced bananas into lemon juice to keep them from turning dark.
- Let vanilla filling cool completely before adding sliced bananas.
- **Note →** Add raw coconut to vanilla pie filling while the filling is hot. The heat will cause the coconut oil to release its flavor into the filling. Sprinkle raw coconut over the meringue before browning. The lightly browned coconut will give more flavor to your coconut cream pie.
- Using canned lemon pie filling is a quick and easy way to make lemon meringue pie. Just put the filling in a pre-baked pie shell, top with meringue, brown and serve. Always use the zest of a fresh lemon in scratch lemon pie filling.
- **Note →** Bake Lemon or Lime cream pies made with Sweetened and Condensed milk for exactly sixteen minutes at 350 degrees. Cool completely before adding topping. Lemon and Lime refrigerator pies will be perfect every time.
- Always let vanilla cream filling cool to room temperature before adding fresh fruit. Hot filling will draw out the water from fresh fruit and cause the filling to separate.
- Bananas, vanilla wafers and cream filling make an ever popular dessert. Display and

serve from a cobbler pan. Layer cream filling, vanilla wafers, sliced bananas in that order until the pan is full. Place vanilla wafers side-by-side flat over the top or cover with a baked meringue.

CUSTARD TYPE PIES

Egg custard pies are best when baked in a crust that has been partially pre-baked. They should be baked at about 300 degrees in a water bath. (Set the pie in a pan containing a little over one-forth inch of water.)

Pumpkin pies and *sweet potato pies* are best baked at a high temperature (425 degrees) for about 15 minutes then at a lower temperature (375 degrees) until they are done.

Chess type pies such as Pecan pie should be baked at 300 degrees for about one hour and twenty to thirty minutes.

Pecan pie bakes best at a low temperature. Chocolate morsels and/or a little coconut make a delicious addition to pecan pie. Bake normally.

WHIPPED CREAM PIES

Use whipped topping rather than fresh whipping cream in whipped cream pies. Whipped topping will hold up better and tastes as good as fresh whipping cream.

Always let cream filling cool completely before adding the filling to the whipped topping. Warm filling may not break the whipped topping down completely, but the heat may hurt the texture. Try mixing peanut butter and vanilla pie filling together then fold the mixture to whipped topping. A peanut butter whipped cream pie is delicious.

COBBLERS

Spray or paint a diluted solution of water and milk then sprinkle a coating of granulated sugar on top of a cobbler's crust. Since there is more filling and less crust in a serving of cobbler; make sure the spices are correct in matching the fruit filling.

Pastry crust is always a major part of the dessert and less of it demands that you are perfect in presenting the cobbler's filling. If possible, make cobblers in half-pans rather than full pans. Each dessert will have a better filling and crust combination when done this way.

Make cobblers out of (two crust) pies that may be under-baked or have boiled over too much. Take off the top crust and use the filling and broken up bottom crust for the cobbler filling. This will save losing the two crust pie.

PUFF PASTRY

Fruit filled turn-overs and small puff pastries for parties can easily be made from pre-made frozen or refrigerated dough. Making puff pastry from scratch is not really difficult, but requires a lot of time. Pre-made raw pastry dough is just as good.

PUFF PASTRY TIPS

- Let puff pastry relax for a few minutes after making it up and before baking. Do not let puff pastry warm to room temperature before baking.

Note

- Bake puff pastry quickly in a fairly hot oven (375 to 400 degrees). Bake until the center is completely done. Raw puff pastry is doughy and must be baked until flaky to be good.
- Use canned fruit pie filling to fill turn-overs. A high quality fruit preserve is also a good filling.
- Always use water to brush on puff pastry. Milk or egg wash will cause the pastry to burn.

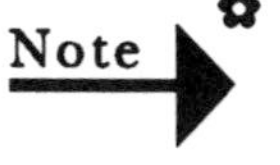

- Drizzle a powdered sugar/water icing over-baked puff pastry for needed sweetness. Use vanilla extract along with fruit flavored extracts or liqueur for flavor.

PUDDINGS

Puddings are cooked the same as cream pie fillings, but puddings are usually much softer. Use the same techniques for making pudding as for pie fillings except use less thickener. Puddings must stand alone for taste, so use a mixture of milk and cream instead of just milk in the mix.

TIPS ON MAKING PUDDINGS

- Do not over-cook pudding mixes. Overcooking will make pudding too thick and may cause it to crack on top.
- Cook all pudding in a double boiler or use a thick sided pot and cook over a very low heat. Stir frequently in either case.
- Add any extracts after the pudding is removed from the heat. Extract flavor is lost in cooking.

- Always place a thin plastic film cover on top of the pudding dishes when they cool to room temperature and before refrigerating them.
- Top with whipped cream just before serving.

INGREDIENTS FOR PIES

SUGAR: Granulated sugar is best to use in most fruit and cream pies. Granulated sugar is also best to use in meringues. Brown sugar is best to use in Pecan pies.

FLOUR: All-purpose flour is good to use in pie crusts. *Pastry flour* is best.

SHORTENING: Chilled all-purpose shortening or hydrogenated is best to use in pie crusts. Butter or margarine is good to use in all sorts of fillings.

FRUIT: Always use ripe fruit in making pies. Over-ripe or green fruit will affect the taste and texture of the filling. Frozen fruit is excellent to use for pie baking. Thaw it completely and drain off all the juice. Canned fruit is also very good in pies. Most canned fruit is packed in syrup and must be drained. Canned prepared fruit pie filling is the easiest solution to making a fruit pie filling. Many fruit choices are available and all are good. Sometimes you may use the juice instead of water, if the recipe calls for water. Frozen fruit is very fragile and must be handled with care to prevent crushing.

MILK: Powdered milk is good to use in pie crusts. Milk helps the crust brown and gives it a better flavor. Fresh milk is good to use in cream filling instead of water. Evaporated milk will give cream filling a rich taste.

EGGS: Fresh, clean eggs should always be used in pie making. Separate the eggs while they are cold, but it's best to let the whites come to room temperature before whipping. Be careful with egg whites, they must be kept in a grease free environment if they are to be whipped.

SALT: Salt is important to flavor enhancement. Salt must be used in pie crust, but is not necessary in fillings.

THICKENERS: Corn starch, eggs, all-purpose flour and gelatin are commonly used thickeners for pie filling. Corn starch and all-purpose flour are usually used to thicken fruit pie fillings. Gelatin is used for whipped cream and chiffon type pies.

CHEESE: Cream cheese is the most commonly used cheese for pie fillings. Make sure the cheese is fresh and not watery.

CREAM: Heavy cream is whipped for toppings, or whipped and folded into other ingredients for whipped cream pies. Light cream is usually spooned over hot pie portions for serving. Cream must be fresh. Look at the date on the container.

SPICES: Cinnamon, allspice, clove, nutmeg and ginger are the most popular spices for pies. Make sure that the spice you use is fresh. Spice loses flavor with age, especially when not sealed properly.

CHOCOLATE: Mix cocoa with salad oil or melted butter before using to flavor cream pies. Melted pure chocolate morsels are also good to use. Melted bitter chocolate baking squares are best to use in chocolate flavored pies. Chocolate absorbs odors and should be fresh. Chocolate will have a bad flavor when not stored properly.

COCONUT: Use fresh, moist coconut in cream pies. Lightly toast a small portion of the coconut and mix with coconut filling to enhance the taste. Add the raw coconut while the cream filling is hot to release the flavor.

NUTS: Nut-meats should always be fresh. They go rancid quickly and should be tasted before using in a filling.

SYRUP: Honey, molasses, light corn syrup and dark corn syrup are the most popular syrups used in pie fillings.

JUICE: Whenever possible use fruit juice instead of water when making fruit pie filling. Canned apple juice will enhance the flavor of almost all fruit fillings.

FLAVOR: Vanilla is the most popular flavor used in pie fillings. Use fresh fruit juice when possible to flavor pie fillings. Lemon, lime and orange juice makes for a tangy flavor that no artificial flavor can compare.

Watching the time is important in baking. Always pay close attention to your mixing time, baking time and even the time you let things cool. Perfectly baked items are not made by accident.

Chapter 6

SAUCES

Contents

CHAPTER SIX

SAUCES

Sauces are an important part of baking and are easy to make. Brush on, pour on or dip fruit into liqueur flavored sauces and add moisture plus unique flavor to pound cake and cake layers.

- Make sure that the tools you use are clean and your ingredients are fresh.
- Pour thick fruit or chocolate sauce over cake/ice cream combinations to make special desserts.
- Mix thin sauces with fresh fruit to sweeten and enhance their natural fruit flavor. Whipped cream sauce makes any dessert even better.

We selected the following sauce recipes with you in mind. We considered their ease of preparation and reasonable cost. We included some simple tips to help get you started in the right direction.

Remember, any recipe is only a guide. Your kitchen's baking conditions and you are unique. Some changes will almost always occur.

Often forgotten, sauces may be used to enhance almost all of your favorite recipes.

TIPS AND RECIPES

SIMPLE SYRUP SAUCE

Simple syrup is a sauce made by boiling together twice as much granulated sugar as water. Example: Boil together 1 pound of granulated sugar with 1 cup of water. Simple syrup can be flavored with any extract or liqueur. Simple syrup is the best sauce to brush or spoon over cake layers and pound cakes. Always brush or spoon on the simple syrup mixture while it is very hot. The hot syrup will easily penetrate the cake and make it deliciously moist and flavorful. Melt *cinnamon candy* in 1 cup of simple syrup to make a super sauce for apple pie.

APRICOT SAUCE

Boil 8 to 12 ounces of apricot jam with a little simple syrup. Push the boiled mixture through a sieve and add Kirsch, Cognac or Rum for flavor.

CHOCOLATE SAUCE

Melt 8 ounces of sweet chocolate in a double boiler or microwave, then slowly add enough fresh whipping cream (stirring as you add the cream) to make the chocolate sauce as thick or thin as you want. Use this sauce to drizzle over pound cake.

Melt 8 ounces of semi-sweet chocolate bar with 1 tablespoon of powdered sugar and 2 ounces of butter. Let this mixture cool a little, then stir in a bit of vanilla and egg yolk until the sauce is as thick as you like. This chocolate sauce must be refrigerated and makes an excellent ice cream topping. (Warm for use.) Use a little orange liqueur for flavor.

Melt 4 ounces of sweet chocolate with 2 tablespoons of light corn syrup to 120 degrees (no more). Add enough simple syrup to make a very thick sauce, then stir in a few drops of vanilla and 3/4 pint of fresh whipping cream. Use this sauce to top off your favorite pudding, ice cream or cake.

LEMON AND ORANGE SAUCE

To 2 cups of vanilla pie filling add a generous amount of finely shredded lemon or orange zest. Slowly, stir in fresh whipping cream until the sauce is as thick as you like. Fruit flavored liqueur will improve the flavor.

MARASCHINO SAUCE

To 2 cups of vanilla cream filling add fresh whipping cream to get the desired thickness. Stir in enough finely chopped maraschino cherries to make the color and taste you like. Add a little kirsch for flavor. Always top this sauce with toasted almonds.

CHANTILLY SAUCE

Lightly whip 1 pint of fresh whipping cream, 4 tablespoons of fine granulated sugar and 1 tablespoon of vanilla to the consistency you like.

COFFEE SAUCE

Boil together: 8 ounces of water, 3 tablespoons of light corn syrup, and 1 teaspoon of vanilla. Remove from the heat and stir in 4 ounces of ground coffee. Let this mixture cool to room temperature. Strain through a coffee strainer and add 4 tablespoons of fine granulated sugar. Stir until the sugar is dissolved, then add and mix in 1 pint of fresh whipping cream.

MELBA SAUCE

Crush 1 pint of fresh raspberries and force them through a sieve. Add 4 ounces of powdered sugar and the juice from 1/2 a lemon. Stir together until the sugar has dissolved.

STRAWBERRY SAUCE

Push 1 pint of ripe strawberries through a sieve. (Frozen strawberries are fine to use.) Stir in 8 ounces of powdered sugar and the juice of 1/2 lemon. Mix together until the sugar has dissolved completely.

ORANGE SYRUP

Cook the juice from 15 very large oranges and the juice from 2 lemons with the shredded zest from 2 oranges with 1 pound 10 ounces of granulated sugar. Heat to 140 degrees and the sugar is dissolved. Do not allow to boil. Strain through cloth and cool completely before bottling. This is an excellent syrup to heat and brush on chocolate cake layers for extra flavor and moisture.

SIMPLE GLAZE RECIPES

Glaze adds shine to your baked desserts. Glazes are easy to make and will give that little extra to make your baking projects special.

HONEY GLAZE

Mix together until smooth: 1 pound of powdered sugar, 4 tablespoons of honey, 1/4 cup of very hot water and 1 teaspoon of vanilla. Brush this glaze over hot sweet rolls, cinnamon rolls and sweet breads. Brush on top of pie crust after baking to make it shine.

JELLY GLAZE

Heat your favorite jelly until it melts then brush over fruitcake for shine. Brush hot jelly over pound cakes to seal in their moisture. Apple or Mint jellies make excellent glazes.

BUN GLAZE

Whisk together: 2 parts fresh egg to 1 part water and a pinch of salt. Brush over crusty breads before baking to make the crust have a bright shine.

TOOLS FOR SAUCE

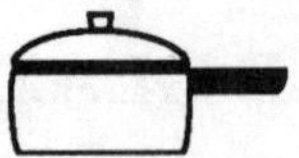

- A thick sided pot or double boiler—at least the 2 quart size (a 3 and 4 quart double boiler is better).
- A large metal bowl for heating water and for chilling sauces.
- A candy thermometer (optional).
- A wire whisk or large spoon for stirring the sauce while it is heating.
- A source of heat from a gas stove, electric stove or microwave oven.
- Glass containers with tight fitting lids to hold the finished sauce, (glass is best because it may be used to warm the sauce).
- A mixer to whip whipping cream.

SOLUTIONS

- ✤ When the sauce you have refrigerated forms sugar crystals you must heat gently over hot water or use the lowest setting on the microwave. Stir slowly while heating and the sugar will dissolve.
- ✤ Heat chocolate sauce (that becomes hard from refrigeration) in your microwave or place its container in a bowl of hot water and let it melt slowly.
- ✤ Fresh fruit and whipping cream sauces will spoil in a few days and should be used as quickly as possible.
- ✤ Always check the *pull* date on whipping cream and use it before that time expires to insure freshness.
- ✤ Try your sauces over pancakes and waffles for a fresh new taste.
- ✤ Pour a cinnamon sauce (simple syrup and cinnamon candy melted together) over baked apples or apple dumplings.

INGREDIENTS

SUGAR: Granulated sugar is best unless the recipe calls for another kind.

SPICE: All spices should be fresh and less used is best.

CREAM: Whipping cream should be bought with a long pull date. It should be kept chilled before and during whipping. Chill the mixing bowl and beaters before whipping cream for greatest volume.

FRESH FRUIT: Usually it is best to cook the fruit before using, but putting it through a food processor will make it perfect for sauces and the flavor is better.

FROZEN FRUIT: Use frozen blueberries and strawberries in sauces over ice cream. Thaw the blueberries, but chop up the strawberries while they are frozen before adding them to the sauce.

FLAVORS: Use emulsion based flavors when possible. Fruit extracts are good also.

LIQUEURS: Use your favorite liqueurs to flavor sauces. These flavors are strong so be careful and not over power the dessert flavor.

FRUIT JUICE: Use fruit juice instead of water whenever possible. Apple juice is excellent to use in almost all fruit based sauce.

Chapter 7

HEALTH

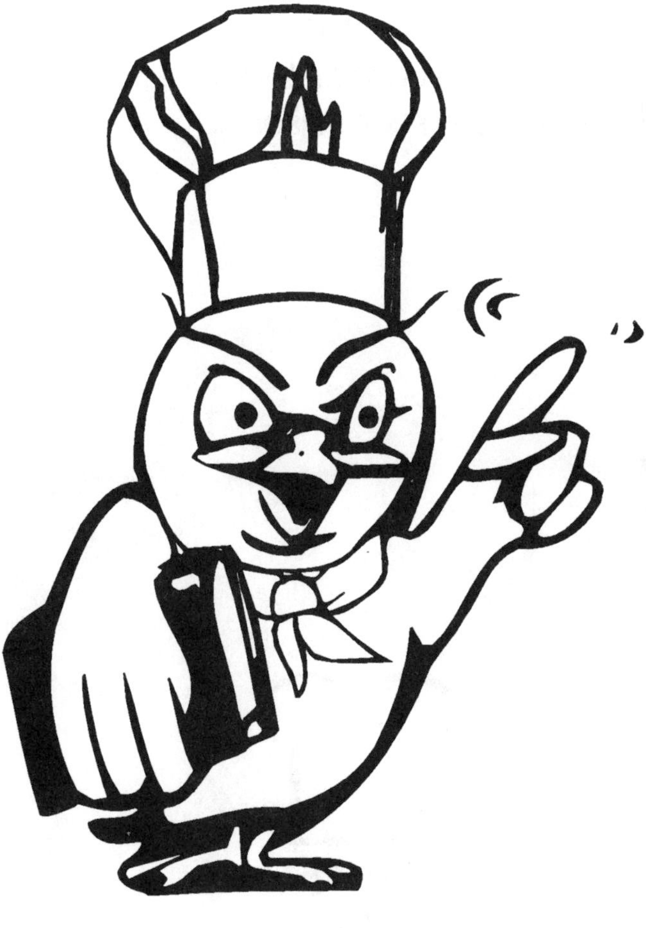

Chapter Seven——Health

Contents

Chapter Seven

HEALTH

This chapter deals with proper food handling and keeping. Everyone worries about their waistlines, but not much is said about doing the things necessary for safe food preparation. We stressed throughout this book about using fresh, high quality ingredients and now We'll tell you how to keep them safe to eat. This chapter may be the most important one in this book. Reading it will make you aware of the dangers to you and your family from unsafe food preparation methods.

Food poisoning is very common and it should be the responsibility of everyone who prepares food to do all they can to prevent poisonings themselves, their families and friends.

Foodborne Illnesses

Almost all foodborne illnesses are caused by bacteria. However, viruses, protozoa and trichinae are other microorganisms that may cause illnesses.

BACTERIA

Bacteria are single celled organisms that take in food, produce waste and multiply very quickly. There are many kinds of bacteria but we'll only tell you about the bad guys.

Pathogenic bacteria is a group name for the bacteria that are capable of causing illness. This group of bacteria may cause illness from living and multiplying in food or they may use food (without growing in it) as the means in which they are transmitted to humans.

Some bacteria produce toxins in foods as they multiply. This toxin is very powerful and will cause illness and even death. Botulinum toxin is the worst and most deadly. *Other toxins will cause various degrees of illness which are almost always thought to be something other than food poisoning.*

Bacteria must have food, moisture and warmth to multiply. Some bacteria must also have air, but others do better without air. All the bacteria that cause foodborne illness prefer foods of a proteinaceous nature such as milk, meat poultry, eggs and seafood. All the bacteria must have moisture to grow. Dry foods such as sugar, flour, cookies and dry baked goods are not good media for bacterial growth. All bacteria grow best at a warm temperature of from 60 to 120 degrees F. Pathogens, the foodborne illness causing bacteria, grow best at about body temperature.

Any food prepared within the temperature range of 45 to 140 degrees F is a possible source of bacterial infection. If the food remains within this temperature range for 2 to 4 hours it may be contaminated and could cause illness.

Bacteria can be killed by heat. However, clostridium botulinum bacteria will survive unless processing methods are followed to the letter. This bacteria grows best without air in a sealed can or jar. Cooking or baking does not mean that food is free from infection. Freezing will not kill bacteria. Bacteria will not grow when frozen, but will continue to grow when the food is thawed.

STAPH FOOD POISONING

The toxin produced by the bacteria staphylococcus aureus (staph) is the most common cause of food poisoning. The staph bacteria grows well in high salt concentrations and in high sugar concentrations. It will also survive freezing. Since it is the toxin that is poison and not the bacteria itself—food poisoning may occur even after the bacteria has been killed by heat.

Symptoms in people who have staph poisoning will appear on an average of 2—3 hours and include salivation, nausea, vomiting, abdominal cramps, diarrhea, headaches, muscular cramps, sweating, chills, and prostration. These symptoms may last for 1—2 days.

The most common source of staph bacteria is the human body. Even healthy people carry the bacteria in their mouths, throats, noses, pimples, and infected wounds. When an infected person does not use proper food handling techniques they may transfer the staph bacteria to food.

Staph is transmitted by

- The infected person passing the staph bacteria to the food.
- The staph bacteria grows and produces the toxin.

- The toxin causes food poisoning in everyone who eats it.

Foods which are most likely to become infected with staph bacteria are those containing protein such as meat, milk, poultry, eggs, fish and shellfish. Foods that are ground or chopped such as ground meat are contaminated from the food handler, tables, equipment. *Eggs used in a recipe could be contaminated if they were held in a bowl which had been used to hold contaminated ground meat, etc.*

Foods contaminated with staph bacteria usually look, smell, and taste normal.

Staph bacteria can be killed by heating to 165 degrees F, but the toxin it has produced will still cause food poisoning.

The best way to prevent staph bacteria food poisoning.

- Keep food clean and free of the bacteria in the first place.

- Keep the food hot at least 140 degrees F or cold at least 45 degrees F.
- Cool cooked or baked food rapidly to a safe temperature.
- Do not sneeze or cough on food.
- Do not touch your nose or mouth while preparing food.
- Keep all sores, cuts and infections treated

and covered while preparing food.

- Sanitize the work table and the tools used.

"Everyone may get poisoned by food if you don't follow common sense rules. Cleanliness is the key to good health—make it an everyday practice."

SALMONELLA FOOD POISONING

Salmonellosis is the infection caused by the salmonella bacteria. This bacteria does not form a toxin and must be ingested in order to cause food poisoning.

The symptoms in people who have salmonellosis are much like staph poisoning except they take an average of 12—24 hours to appear.

Salmonella bacteria come from:

- The intestinal tract of humans.
- Human feces and sewage.
- The intestinal tract of animals.
- Animal feces and sewage.

Salmonella bacteria can be killed by heating food to 165 degrees F. However, foods may be contaminated after cooking and therefore the following precautions are a must.

- Everyone should wash and dry their hands before handling food.

- Everyone should wash and dry their hands after visiting the toilet.
- Everyone should wash and dry their hands after handling raw meat.
- Work area surfaces should be scrubbed and sanitized before and after using for the

preparation of foods.

- Rodents and insects must be kept under control.
- Pets must not be allowed in the kitchen.
- Keep foods hot at 140 degrees F and cold at 45 degrees F.
- Plumbing should be kept in good working order to prevent contamination from sewage.
- **Note** → Cracked or dirty eggs should never be used.
- Poultry should be rinsed well and cooked at a high temperature.
- All meat (especially ground and rolled) and fish should be cooked well.

PERFRINGENS FOOD POISONING

Clostridium perfringens causes gastrointestinal illness. In perfringens poisoning toxin and large numbers of the bacterial cells must be ingested.

Perfringens are found everywhere. They are in the intestinal tract of humans and animals, feces, sewage, manure, soil and dust.

Symptoms occur within 8—22 hours and are much the same as those of staph except usually no vomiting.

Perfringens may be controlled by

- Use separate work surfaces for raw meats and other menu items.
- Wash your hands after handling raw meat.
- Wash your hands after visiting the toilet.
- Keep your kitchen dust free.
- Do not handle cooked meat after handling raw meat.
- Keep food hot at 140 degrees F and cold at 45 degrees F.
- Cool hot foods as rapidly as possible and do not let set at room temperature.

SOLUTIONS

Here is a list of things that will prevent food poisoning:

- Do not reuse containers or use containers for something other than which they are intended. (Do not use a salt shaker to hold anything other than salt.)
- Never store caustic materials in the kitchen.
- Keep flies and other insects out of the kitchen.
- Get rid of rusted cans, swollen cans and dented cans. Do not feed their contents to your pets.
- Get rid of home canned products that are not fresh. (The canning recipe should tell you the maximum time to keep an item.)
- Follow home canning methods to the letter.
- Do not keep anything that is molded.
- Sanitize your work area and inside your refrigerator regularly.
- Keep your glasses, plates, utensils clean and dust free. (Wash and rinse in very hot water.)
- Do not store pesticides near foods.

- Keep the floors, walls and ceiling of your kitchen clean and dust free.
- Store dry foods in a clean, insect free place. Do not store near water pipes or under sewer pipes.
- All opened packages should be stored in closed and labeled containers.
- Always use the oldest packages first. Put fresh boxes and cans to the back of the storage shelf.

Note

- Check and make sure that your refrigerator is at 40 degrees F or below. Make sure your freezer is at 0 degrees F.
- Allow for good air circulation around items in your refrigerator.
- Divide large quantities of food into small sizes for faster cooling.
- Date everything in your freezer and use the oldest first.
- Keep garbage areas out of the kitchen.
- Keep screens on doors and windows in good condition. Seal cracks and holes in walls. Use pest controls regularly and safely.
- Keep your dishwasher clean and in good running order.
- Insist that everyone maintains good personal hygiene.

Preventing food poisoning may seem like a lot of work, but you should realize that the contamination is always present. Your sense of responsibility is the only thing that will keep it from hurting you and others.

Chapter 8 KITCHEN Hints

Chapter Eight——Kitchen Hints

Contents

CHAPTER EIGHT

KITCHEN HINTS

This chapter contains various tips and hints that didn't make it in the other chapters and some we thought were worth repeating.

Many times we've started a baking project and found that we didn't have all the tools or ingredients for it. We've had to make do with whatever was at hand. Hopefully you will find some of our make-shift ideas useful.

BREADS & BISCUITS

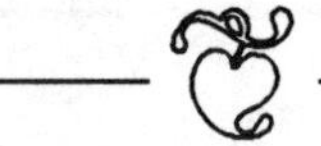

❖ Brush melted butter over the tops of breads and biscuits as soon as they are removed from the oven. This will make the crust soft and full of flavor.

❖ Mix a pinch of salt with one egg and brush over biscuits (scratch or pre-made) before baking to make a beautiful golden crust with a hint of egg flavor.

❖ Add a little food coloring to the bread mix with the water and give your party sandwiches some pizzazz.

❖ Freeze bread before cutting it into small sandwich shapes so that the edges will not be smashed. Cut one slice at a time because it will thaw quickly.

❖ Use dry (instant) yeast instead of fresh to reduce rising time. This reduction in time will eliminate a lot of your kitchen environment problems.

❖ Wrap a canned ham in Rye bread dough and bake the ham as usual. Mix the dough with extra water so that it is loose and do not let it rise. Roll it flat and big enough to completely cover the ham. After baking remove and discard the dough.

❖ Put a cake pan about half full of water in the oven while baking bread. This will provide enough moisture to keep the crust from drying out too much.

❖ Bake biscuits at a high temperature and use two pans under them to keep their bottoms from burning.

❖ Freeze stale bread and then make croutons by cutting it into small cubes. Toast the bread cubes until they are crispy. Brush bread slices with melted butter and sprinkle on garlic or onion powder before cutting into cubes.

Note → ❖ Cut stale bread into small pieces and feed it to wild birds.

❖ Chop up stale bread and biscuits—sprinkle with garlic powder and add to dog food. They love the flavor and it's good for them.

❖ Always place bread and rolls seam down in the baking pan.

❖ Never use hot water in a bread recipe—it will kill the yeast.

❖ When your bread rises too fast or is full of big holes you must add less yeast. (25 to 50 percent) The rising area may be too warm. The liquid in the dough may be too warm.

❖ When your bread rises too slow you must make sure the yeast is fresh, the water is warm, the rising area is at least 80 degrees, the dough is not too stiff.

CAKES & FROSTINGS

- When the topping for pineapple upside down cake gets too dark before the cake is done you should set the cake pan on a cookie sheet for baking. This extra thickness on the bottom will protect and keep the brown sugar mixture and the pineapple a perfect color.

- **Note** If butter-cream frosting is too thick, use a little milk to thin it or warm in the microwave for a few seconds. Icing a cake sometimes is a difficult task and it's very important to use butter-cream at a soft consistency.

- Chill cake layers before applying the frosting if they seem too soft and crumbly. It's not a good idea to ice frozen layers because sometimes water will form on the outside of the finished frosting.

- Place a high quality fruit preserve in your blender or food processor and mix until smooth. This only takes a few seconds to do. Use the mixture as a spread between the layers or on top of your cake. You may also add a little of the mixture to butter-cream frosting to give it a fruit color and flavor.

- Mix cocoa with melted butter or margarine to make a thick, smooth paste. Use this paste to change white butter-cream into chocolate butter-cream frosting. Sometimes just adding cocoa to white butter-cream will cause lumps of cocoa that will not mix out.

❖ You don't always have to coat a greased pan with flour. Cakes that have a high sugar content must be coated, but many others do not. Use cocoa to coat a chocolate cake pan for a little more flavor and to eliminate the color of the flour.

❖ Butter or margarine may be used to coat cake pans, but all-purpose shortening is economical and does not burn like butter or margarine. A spray release agent that contains flour is a perfect choice for most recipes. *Lightly dust with flour or cocoa after using a spray release that does not contain flour.*

❖ Cheese cakes are sometimes difficult to cut cleanly. To cut a cheese cake properly, use a thin blade knife that has been moistened with a warm, wet towel. Push the blade length wise into the cake and pull straight out from the bottom (do not lift the blade up.) Clean and moisten the blade with the towel before each cut.

COOKIES & BROWNIES

- Chill cookie dough about 15 to 30 minutes before making into cookies.
- Put only enough flour on your work surface and rolling pin to prevent sticking. Excess flour may cause the cookies to be hard.
- **Note** → Use an ice cream scoop to drop cookies. Your cookies will all be the same size and will bake evenly. If the dough is sticky dip the scoop into water between scoops.
- Cut cookies as close together as possible. Gently work the remaining dough back into the fresh dough.
- Use a salt shaker to sprinkle sugar on top of cookies. This looks better and is not as messy as using your hand.
- Drizzle a warm powdered sugar/milk glaze over cookies for extra sweetness. Color it a bit and sprinkle on decorettes to make them pretty.

MUFFINS

❖ Almost any Quick bread can be also used to make muffins. Instead of making into loaves just put the batter into muffin cups and bake at a slightly higher temperature (about 10 degrees).

❖ Muffins freeze well, so it is best to freeze them and re-heat in the microwave or oven as needed.

❖ When adding fresh fruit to muffin batter either cut back on the recipe's liquid or drain off excess fruit juice. Crushed strawberries are wonderful used in muffins but will make the batter too thin if you do not adjust for their extra juice.

❖ Use apple juice instead of water in your muffin recipe.

❖ Quick nut breads will almost always crack on the top of the loaf while baking. Don't worry—it's normal.

PIES & FILLINGS

❖ Place pie dough between sheets of waxed paper when rolling out.

❖ Always use eggs at room temperature. Never let them set out too long because they may spoil. The best way to quickly warm eggs is to place them (unbroken) in a dish of warm water for a few minutes.

❖ When adding eggs to a cooked filling, always add a little of the hot filling to the egg mixture. Stir it in before you add them to the total mixture. Eggs cook very quickly. If added to a boiling mixture they sometimes will cook into tiny lumps rather than blend into the filling. Since they are used as a thickener the filling will be lumpy and runny.

❖ If your pie crust takes too long to brown and the filling boils out, add a little milk powder and sugar to the dough recipe the next time you make it. The crust will taste better and will brown quickly.

❖ Cover the top of a fruit pie with an empty pie tin while baking to keep the top crust from browning before the bottom crust is done.

❖ Brush hot apple jelly or a honey/water glaze over the baked fruit pie crust to make it shine.

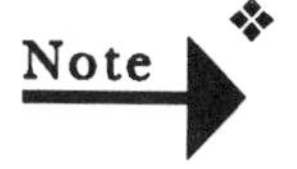

❖ Keep your pie crust from becoming soggy when baking fruit and custard pies by pre-baking them. Paint an egg wash mixture on the bottom of the pie crust and bake at 375 degrees for about 5 minutes. The crust will still look raw, but it will be baked enough to prevent it from becoming soggy.

❖ When using graham crackers or vanilla wafers for a crumb crust you'll need 1 1/2 cups of crumbs. That is about 20 graham cracker squares or about 45 vanilla wafers.

MERINGUE TIPS

A simple **soft** meringue is made by whipping egg whites with a little granulated sugar, vanilla and a bit of cream of tartar. This slightly sweet topping is heaped over a cream pie and then lightly browned for a finishing touch. A perfect soft meringue will be light and airy with no signs of shrinking.

A **hard** meringue contains more sugar and is baked at a very low temperature or allowed to dry at room temperature until it is solid (crispy). Meringue shells, fruit cups and cookies are made from hard meringue.

❖ Meringue will not tolerate even the smallest amount of fat. Since egg yolk contains fat—separating the whites from the yolks must be done carefully. The mixing bowl and the beaters must also be fat free. Wash them in hot soapy water and rinse in hot water before using to make meringue. *Do this for Angel food cake meringue also.*

Note: *Plastic bowls will sometime hold fats even after machine washing. Always use glass or metal bowls for holding meringues.*

❖ Adding the granulated sugar as the egg whites are beating should be done very slowly so it will dissolve completely.

❖ Meringue is ready when the sugar is dissolved and the mixture stands up to a peak when the beaters are lifted.

❖ Spread the meringue over the pie filling making sure it touches the pie crust all around. This will minimize shrinking and slipping.

❖ Brown meringue at a high temperature for only a few minutes (385—400 degrees) until the peaks are lightly brown. If using a low temperature the meringue will have a thick crust and be difficult to cut.

❖ Hard meringues require the same handling techniques as soft meringues. They should be allowed to dry completely before adding the filling.

❖ Make little cups from hard meringue, fill them with fresh fruit and top with whipped cream or whipped topping for something special. **Note:** Fill the cups just before serving because the meringue will become soggy fast.

❖ Fold chopped pecans into hard meringue and spread it about 1/4 inch thick on parchment paper on which you have drawn 5—eight-inch circles. These flat meringues dry in a 200 degree oven for about three hours. Stack them with a thick filling of whipped topping between each layer and then ice the outside with whipped topping and sprinkle with shaved chocolate. Freeze this (cake) first, then cut it while it is still very cold. It is sweet beyond compare, but many people think it is the best dessert ever.

❖ Use **MERINGUE POWDER** in recipes calling for egg whites if you fear salmonella. Two teaspoons of meringue powder dissolved in two tablespoons of warm water equals one egg white. You can find meringue powder at your bakery/restaurant supply store or from popular mail order houses.

SAUCES

❖ Melt chocolate chips and a little whipping cream together in your microwave or over a hot water bath. Add enough cream to thin the melted chocolate just enough to pour. Remove from the heat and gently stir in an egg yolk to make the mixture have a glossy finish. If the mixture is too thick add whipping cream a little at a time until it is right. The egg yolk must be at room temperature before adding or else it will cause the chocolate to set. (*always use clean, uncracked eggs*)

Note ❖ A simple fruit syrup sauce of twice as much sugar as water (two cups sugar plus one cup water) is easy to make—just boil together. Add lots of chopped fresh fruit while the sauce is hot and make a delicious sauce for pouring over ice cream or adding a little extra to your cake layers.

❖ Use sweetened whipping cream (without whipping) as a sauce to pour over cake slices, brownies and warm slices of pie. It's delicious.

HELPFUL SOLUTIONS

- Use the top of a small juice glass or jar to cut out cookies and biscuits. Dip cutting edge into flour between cuts to prevent sticking.
- Use a warm oven (80 to 90 degrees) for a place to let bread rise. Always place a pan half full of water in also to provide the needed moisture.
- A glass bottle makes a perfect stand to hold an inverted angle food cake while it is cooling.

- There are two kinds of measuring cups. One is for measuring dry ingredients and has a round top. The other is for measuring liquids and has a lip for pouring. Be sure to use the correct cup for the job or else the measurement will be wrong.
- Use glass containers and thin aluminum pans to bake in, but reduce the baking temperature about 25 degrees.
- Measure margarine the same as shortening. *If using stick margarine— use these measurements:*

  1/4 stick = 2 tbsp.
  1/2 stick = 4 tbsp. or 1/4 cup
  1 stick = 1/4 pound or 1/2 cup
  4 sticks = 1 pound or 2 cups

- ❖ Use bowls, pans, glasses, cups as molds for baked items or soft molded desserts. Always make sure they are oven or microwave safe.
- ❖ Use a jar filled with water as a rolling pin.
- ❖ Use an ice cream scoop to drop cookies.
- ❖ Punch holes in the lid of a jar and use it to shake sugar over cookies and cakes.
- ❖ Put crackers, cookies and graham crackers between waxed paper and crush with a rolling pin to make crumbs.
- ❖ Place ice cubes in a cloth towel and crush with a hammer or meat mallet.
- ❖ Parchment paper is best, but you may make a cone for decorating out of waxed paper.
- ❖ Wrap a hot towel around a molded dessert dish or cold cake pan for a few seconds to help it release easily.
- ❖ Use a large fork to mix ingredients if your mixer is broken.
- ❖ Use the microwave to quickly heat small amounts of liquids or to melt shortening, chocolate and butter.

Note →

- ❖ Your food processor or blender will make fresh apple sauce in a few seconds. Add spices and create delicious sauce for recipes or eating.
- ❖ Use a piece of clean brown paper from a sack to cover the tops of bread or pies to

keep them from burning.

- ❖ Strain liquids through a clean piece of cloth cut from old sheets or pillow cases.

- ❖ Oven thermometers are inexpensive and come in two types. One kind is used to measure the temperature of the baking item and the other kind is to measure the temperature of the oven—it is a good idea to use both types.

- ❖ Folded cup towels make excellent pot holders.

- ❖ Cake cooling racks come in all sizes and shapes. It is a good plan to have different sizes for each baking project.

- ❖ Place a small juice glass (top-up) in the center of a large cake pan when baking cakes in your microwave (grease or spray with a release agent). Pour the cake batter around the glass and bake as usual. The cake will bake much better.

- ❖ Clean copper bowls with a 50/50 mixture of vinegar and table salt.

- ❖ If the dessert flops, send someone to the bakery and pick up something. *It happens to us all.*

PUDDING

The consistency of puddings depend upon the temperature at which they are served. Some puddings must be served hot or else they will become soggy. Souffles will begin to fall as soon as they are removed from the oven and must be served hot. Other puddings must be chilled almost to the freezing point in order to be correct. Therefore, it is very important to follow the recipe's handling directions to the letter.

- ❖ Keep puddings from forming a crust by covering them with waxed paper or plastic wrap directly on top of the hot surface.
- ❖ Grease molds well before adding the pudding mixture.
- ❖ After chilling, dip the mold in hot water for a few seconds or cover with a hot towel for a few seconds to make the pudding release easily.
- ❖ Add one forth cup pudding to a box of cake mix after it has been mixed for the proper time. Mix the pudding just enough to incorporate into the cake batter. This will make the cake more moist and add a little flavor. It is very important to add the pudding last.

CUSTARDS

Almost all custard failure is a result of cooking too long or cooking at too high of a temperature.

- ❖ When baking in the oven, custard must always be poured into cups and the cups set into a pan of water. Bake in a moderate oven until firm. To test for doneness—insert a knife near the outer edge of the custard. If it comes out clean the custard will be done. Place the cups in cool water to stop the baking process.
- ❖ When cooking custard on top of the stove use a double boiler and medium heat only. If cooked too fast the eggs will lump and will not hold the liquid in suspension as they should. Add about 1/2 cup of the hot liquid to the eggs and stir in before adding the eggs to the mixture. Once the eggs are added—stir constantly until the mixture will coat a metal spoon.

- ❖ Continue to stir custard after it has been removed from the heat in order to release the steam. Set the pan in a bowl of ice water while stirring for best texture.
- ❖ Add bananas, coconut, fruit, nuts after the custard has cooled.
- ❖ Use left-over custard to add moisture to your boxed cake mix. Add 1/4 cup per box. Heat the rest in the microwave and use it to frost the cake.

WHIPPING CREAM

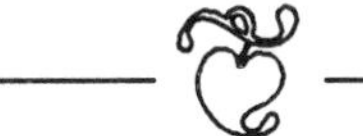

Whipping cream contains 30% milk fat and can be whipped until it doubles in volume. One cup of cream will yield about two cups of whipped cream.

- ❖ Over whipped cream will turn into butter.
- ❖ Always use chilled cream and a chilled bowl/beater. Whipping cream may not whip if it is not cold.

- ❖ Two cups of cream is about the maximum amount to whip at one time.
- ❖ Add two to four tablespoons of sugar per cup of cream to sweeten. Add the sugar when the volume and stiffness is almost complete. If added too soon, the cream may not whip.
- ❖ Add a teaspoon of vanilla per cup for extra flavor.
- ❖ Whipped cream freezes well (up to three months), but should be served/used while still very cold.

INGREDIENTS

SALTED BUTTER may be used in most recipes that call for SWEET BUTTER. There is very little salt in butter and usually you will not notice any difference in the taste of baked items. The salt taste is stronger if salted butter is brushed on a baked item.

HOT WATER is defined as water *very hot to the touch*, but not boiling.

COLD WATER is defined as water *very cold to the touch*, but not ice water.

ICE WATER is defined as water from the refrigerator or water that has been cooled by adding ice to it.

TAP WATER is defined as water at room temperature, *not warm and not cold.*

SPICE (*type-of*) is defined as ground (not whole) unless the recipe specifies differently.

FRUIT may be fresh, frozen or canned. The recipe will usually tell you which to use.

NUTS may be substituted as to what you have on hand or to suit your taste. Walnuts may be substituted for pecans and the recipe will change in taste only.

SUGAR should usually be used as the recipe specifies. Sometimes powdered sugar may be substituted for granulated sugar, but not always. Brown sugar comes in light, medium and dark brown. The type of brown sugar you use will determine the characteristics of the baked item.

SHORTENING should be used as the recipe specifies However, in cookies and in some cakes margarine or butter may be substituted creating a better flavor. Lard is a poor substitute for shortening. With the exception for use in pie dough, should not be used.

MILK should be used as the recipe specifies. Powdered milk may be used in the place of whole milk, but not used to replace cream, condensed or sweetened condensed milk.

FLOUR should be used as the recipe specifies most of the time. *Bread flour* is a good substitute for *all purpose flour* in bread recipes. Cake flour is usually best to use in cake recipes for the best texture. Bleached and unbleached flours are interchangeable in all your recipes.

EGGS should be used always as the recipe specifies. Using two yolks to one white (as a substitute for one egg) will make almost any baked item more moist and richer tasting.

EGG WHITE POWDER: Two teaspoons of egg white powder dissolved in two tablespoons of warm water is equal to one egg white. You may substitute the egg white powder (4 teaspoons powder plus 4 tablespoons water) for one whole egg in almost all baked recipes.

BAKING POWDER should always be fresh and used as the recipe specifies. Almost all modern recipes call for double acting baking powder. However, if you are using a very old recipe, single acting baking powder is best. Make it yourself by sifting together: 2 tablespoons cream of tartar, 1 tablespoon baking soda and 1 tablespoon corn starch. Use exactly what you need and keep the rest stored in a tightly sealed container.

BAKING SODA should always be fresh and used as the recipe specifies.

DUST is an ingredient term usually meaning to use flour on the work surface to keep something from sticking to it. However, it also means to use cookie crumbs, cocoa, or flour to coat the pan grease inside cake pans to prevent the cake batter from sticking to the pan.

YEAST comes in several forms. Always read the directions and check the expiration date before you use these different kinds.

1. Active fresh yeast comes in a one ounce cube and must be refrigerated.

2. Rapid Rise yeast is dried, comes in 1/4 ounce package and does not need refrigeration. This is very fast acting yeast.

3. Active dry yeast comes in 1/4 ounce packages and does not need refrigeration. This yeast has a normal acting time.

COCONUT is easy to color for parties. Place a few drops of food color in 1/2 teaspoon milk and toss with 1 to 1 1/2 cups of coconut using a fork. Toast coconut in your oven for about 7 to 10 minutes at 350 degrees. Stir often.

EMULSIFIED SHORTENING is best to use in scratch cakes and frostings. It is usually not sold in stores and must be bought from your local bakery.

MACAROON COCONUT is great for cookies and to sprinkle as a topping. It is usually not found in stores and must be bought from your local bakery.

ALMOND PASTE makes a wonderful filling, topping and flavor, but is hard to find in stores. It is also very expensive when you are able to find it. Ask your local bakery to sell you some.

FRUIT SPREADS are used in frostings—as frostings, between cake layers and as cookie garnishes. Fruit spreads can be bought from your local bakery in small quantites.

SUGAR SUBSTITUTES may be used in some recipes, but as a rule they do not provide the mass and sturcture of sugar and will not work. Use recipes designed for sugar substitutes. Sugar substitutes will sweeten cream and can be used to sprinkle over desserts to cut calories a little.

MICROWAVE HINTS

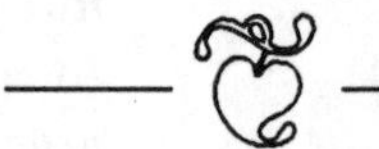

Defrosting pies in the microwave is quick and easy. A frozen **fruit pie** will take 4 to 5 minutes on DEFROST with about 5 minutes of standing time to defrost.

❖ A frozen **cream pie** will take about 1 1/2 minutes on DEFROST with about 5 minutes of standing time to defrost.

SPECIAL NOTE: ALWAYS REMOVE THE PIE FROM ITS METAL PAN AND PLACE IT IN A GLASS OR PAPER PAN BEFORE PUTTING IT INTO YOUR MICROWAVE. USING METAL OF ANY KIND IN A MICROWAVE IS DANGEROUS AND MAY RUIN YOUR OVEN.

❖ A frozen **layer cake** will take about 2 minutes and 5 minutes standing time to defrost. Use the SIMMER setting.

NOTE: *Leave the cake in its package for defrosting unless there is metal in the package. If there is metal in the package—remove the metal and then defrost the cake.*

❖ Defrost packages (boxes) of **frozen fruit** for 5 minutes on the DEFROST setting. Let stand for about 1 minute before removing from the package. Pouches of frozen fruit will defrost in about 3 minutes on the DEFROST setting and 1 minute of standing time. These times are variable as is the power of your microwave.

NOTE: *Always use round pans instead of square ones when possible in your microwave. Using round pans will eliminate burned or dry corners.*

- ❖ **SAUCES** are easily prepared in the microwave. Use the microwave setting which seems best for each kind of sauce. Stir the sauce every few seconds and heat to a temperature of 140 to 150 degrees.

NOTE: *Use the microwave to heat up pre-made sauces just before serving and don't worry about over cooking or scorching. Hot chocolate sauce poured over a dish of ice cream and sprinkled with chopped nuts is truly a wonderful thing.*

- ❖ Toast coconut in the microwave. Spread the coconut thinly on a paper plate or towel and use the high setting for 2 or 3 minutes. Watch it closely because it will brown quickly when it starts.

Your Notes

Your plastic spatula is
your friend. Use it often
to scrape the sides of the
mixing bowl when you add
ingredients.

Chapter 9

CHOCOLATE

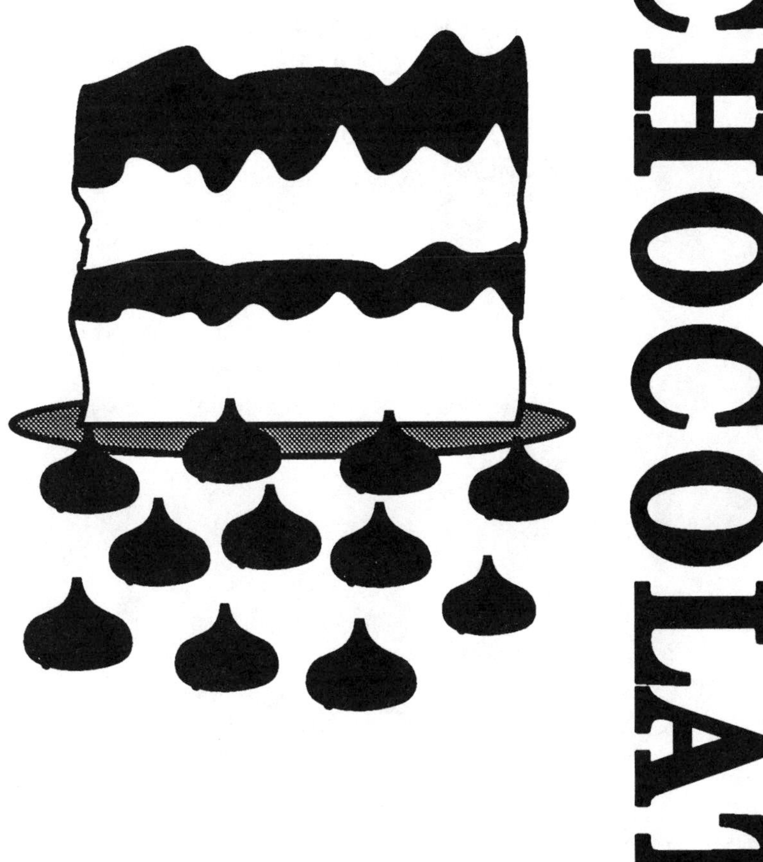

Chapter Nine——Chocolate

Contents

CHAPTER NINE

CHOCOLATE

Chocolate is the most popular flavoring ingredient used in baked products. Chocolate cakes, frostings, cookies, brownies, pies and candy are consumed more than all other flavors combined. Why? Chocolate satisfies the eye as well as the palette. Looking for something sweet and something special—chocolate items satisfy. Chocolate treats are rarely disappointing and therefore they are the first choice to fill a craving for the best.

We have written a little about chocolate in some of our other chapters, but since it plays such a large part in baking we decided to devote a chapter to it.

Chocolate began its rise to fame with Columbus bringing cocoa beans back from the New World. No one knew what the brown beans were used for until Cortez brought cocoa beans from Mexico. The Aztecs made a drink from the cocoa beans and called it "cacahuatl," or "gift from the gods".

The use of the chocolate drink "chocolate" became popular in Europe and spread around the world. During American Revolutionary times chocolate factories sprang up in the United States. In the 1800's Daniel Peter in Switzerland developed a formula for adding milk to basic chocolate and produced the first solid chocolate. American manufactures have since brought chocolate to where it is today.

What is Chocolate?

CACAO (COCOA) BEANS are the beans cocoa is made from. They are grown mainly in West Africa and South America.

COCOA NIBS are the "meat" of the cocoa beans. The whole cocoa bean is roasted and then the outer shell is removed. The nibs are then processed into chocolate products. The nibs contain about 50% cocoa butter.

CHOCOLATE LIQUOR is the base of all chocolate. The nibs are ground at a temperature which causes the cocoa butter to liquefy and creates the liquor or "liquid essence" of the cocoa nibs. There is no alcohol in chocolate liquor.

COCOA BUTTER is the vegetable fat extracted from processing chocolate liquor. Cocoa butter is what gives chocolate products their unique texture.

COCOA POWDER is what is left after the cocoa butter has been taken from the chocolate liquor. Cocoa powder is very low in fat content.

AMERICAN PROCESSED COCOA is a term used for cocoa liquor processed without additives.

DUTCH PROCESSED COCOA is a term used for cocoa liquor processed using an alkali agent. This cocoa is darker than American

Process and has a different flavor.

BITTER CHOCOLATE is pure chocolate liquor and usually formed into bars. It is referred to as Unsweetened, Baking, or Cooking chocolate.

SEMI-SWEET CHOCOLATE is a combination of chocolate liquor, cocoa butter and sugar. Semi-sweet chocolate contains at least 35% chocolate liquor. It comes in bars and chips.

SWEET CHOCOLATE is a combination of chocolate liquor, cocoa butter and sugar. Sweet chocolate contains at least 15% chocolate liquor and has a high sugar content.

MILK CHOCOLATE is a combination of chocolate liquor, cocoa butter, sugar and milk or cream. Milk chocolate contains at least 10% chocolate liquor.

WHITE CHOCOLATE is not chocolate at all.

CHOCOLATE FLAVORED is a term applied to those products that do not contain enough chocolate liquor to meet government standards.

STORING CHOCOLATE

- Chocolate will stay fresh for about a year if it is stored in a cool, dry place. (65°—70° F)

Note → Temperature above 75 degrees will cause chocolate to melt. Cocoa butter comes to the surface and forms a film called "bloom". Sugar may also rise to the surface in the same way. "Bloom" does not affect the quality of the chocolate in any way.

Note → Always package chocolate tightly. Wrap it in foil and place in a resealable plastic bag for best protection.

- If chocolate is exposed to air for a prolonged period of time it will absorb odors and become rancid tasting.

Your Notes

SUBSTITUTING COCOA

Cocoa may be substituted for chocolate in many of your favorite recipes.

- UNSWEETENED BAKING CHOCOLATE: Use 3 level tablespoons of cocoa plus 1 tablespoon of liquid or solid shortening to equal 1 block (1 ounce) of unsweetened baking chocolate.
- LIQUID UNSWEETENED BAKING CHOCOLATE: Use 3 level tablespoons cocoa plus 1 tablespoon oil or melted shortening to equal 1 package (1 ounce).
- SEMI-SWEET CHOCOLATE: Use 6 level tablespoons cocoa plus 7 tablespoons sugar plus 1/4 cup shortening to equal one 6 ounce package (1 cup) of semi-sweet chips.
- SWEET BAKING CHOCOLATE: Use 3 level tablespoons cocoa plus 4 1/2 tablespoons sugar plus 2 2/3 tablespoons shortening to equal one 4 ounce bar of sweet baking chocolate.

CHOCOLATE DECORATIONS

CHOCOLATE CURLS

Chocolate curls are fun to make and add a bunch of eye appeal to your chocolate cakes and pies.

Tools you will need

1. A baking sheet with a very clean bottom.
2. A sharp knife, vegetable peeler or straight-tipped metal spatula.
3. Aluminum foil.
4. Wooden toothpicks.
5. Waxed paper.

Place 2 or 3 squares of semi-sweet or sweet chocolate on a piece of aluminum foil sheet and heat in a warm oven until the chocolate is barely softened.

Use a sharp knife or vegetable peeler to shave the chocolate from the foil. (Hold the knife at a slight angle and scrape along the foil causing the chocolate to curl in front of the knife. Fast movement will cause tight curls and slow movement will cause loose curls.

Lift the curls with a wooden toothpick and place on waxed paper. Chill until ready for use.

ANOTHER METHOD: Melt 4 to 6 ounces of semi-sweet chips or 1 package of sweet chocolate in the microwave. Less heat is best so do not over heat the chocolate. Pour and spread the melted chocolate to a thin layer on the bottom of a baking sheet.

Chill for about 6 to 8 minutes then slip the straight end of a spatula under the chocolate and scrape until a curl forms.

If the chocolate is too soft—chill longer, if it is too cold let stand at room temperature until ready to be worked.

Lift the curls with a wooden toothpick and place on waxed paper. Chill until ready for use. Melt any scraps and use them again.

LEAVES

Melt 4 ounces of semi-sweet chips or 1 bar of sweet chocolate in your microwave or over very low heat stirring constantly.

Spread (paint) the melted chocolate on the underside of washed and dried grape ivy, lemon, rose or gardenia leaves. Form a smooth, thick coat on each leaf then place on a waxed paper lined tray and chill until the chocolate sets (about 12 to 15 minutes.) Peel the leaves from the chocolate and place the chocolate leaves on your dessert.

Use cabbage leaves to make serving size chocolate bowls. Follow the same technique as for small leaves except paint on a coat of chocolate—chill slightly—paint on more chocolate until the chocolate is thick enough to serve as your bowl.

CUT OUTS

Melt 4 ounces of semi-sweet chips or 1 package of sweet chocolate.

Pour on a waxed paper lined tray and spread with a spatula to about a 1/8 inch thickness. Chill about 12 to 15 minutes and cut with a sharp cookie cutter or knife. *Lift at once* from the waxed paper and place on your dessert.

MELTING CHOCOLATE

- Chocolate scorches easily and must be melted with care over very low heat. A microwave is best for melting chocolate, but other heat sources are all right as long as you are very careful.
- Using very low heat on the stove burner melt chocolate in a thick bottomed pan and stir constantly.

- Melt chocolate in a hot water bath by placing a bowl *holding the chocolate* in a large sauce pan filled with about 2 inches of water. The chocolate should be stirred while melting.
- Melt chocolate in your oven by placing it in a cake baking pan and using very low

heat. Remove from the oven as soon as the chocolate is soft.

- For candy dipping always use the hot water method of melting chocolate and remove from the heat before all the chocolate has melted. Stir gently until the remaining chocolate melts and dip the candy.

Note

- All your utensils for melting chocolate must be dry. If even a few drops of moisture gets into the melting chocolate it will become lumpy. Use 1 teaspoon of oil to 1 ounce of chocolate to bring it back to its correct consistency.

- Unsweetened chocolate will change into a liquid when melting. Semi-sweet chocolate and sweet chocolate will hold its shape until it is stirred.

ICE CREAM

Home-made ice cream takes only a few minutes to prepare and is the perfect topping for cakes, brownies and pies. Sure, you can buy almost any flavor you can dream up, but nothing tastes better than fresh ice cream with the special touches you add.

We have selected vanilla and chocolate ice cream recipes so that you may use these as a base and add other flavors and fruits to make many different kinds.

Vanilla ice cream

- Preparation time is about 15 to 20 minutes.
- Cooking time is about 10 minutes for cooking the cream.
- Cooling time is about 30 minutes on ice before freezing.
- Freezing time is about 30 to 45 minutes.

INGREDIENTS for one quart of vanilla ice cream.

Two cups of milk

1 tablespoon of vanilla

1 cup of granulated sugar

6 large egg yolks

1 cup of whipping cream

METHOD

- Place the milk and 1/2 the sugar in a sauce pan and bring to a boil. Remove from the heat, cover the pot and let cool for 10 minutes.
- Place the egg yolks and the remaining 1/2 of the sugar in a bowl and beat with a mixer until thick and light in color.
- Place the milk/sugar mixture back on the heat and bring to a boil. Pour 1/4 cup of this boiling mixture into the egg yolk/sugar mixture. (mixing constantly as the hot liquid is added)
- Remove the sauce pan from the heat and pour the egg mixture into the milk mixture. (stirring constantly with a spoon)
- Place the sauce pan back over very low heat and cook until it thickens. If you use a candy thermometer 185 degrees F. NOTE: Do not bring to a boil. If you do not use a candy thermometer—cook until the mixture coats the spoon and a line drawn across the top of the mixture will keep its form. Cooking time will be about 5 to 10 minutes.
- Remove the cooked cream from the heat and pour into a bowl. Set this bowl in a larger bowl filled with ice cubes to speed the cooling process. Add the whipping

cream and the vanilla to the mixture. Stir it in well. NOTE: The cooked cream must be allowed to cool completely before freezing. (about 30 minutes over ice cubes)

- Add the cream to your ice cream freezer and follow its directions for freezing.

SPECIAL NOTE: If you over cook the cream *and it curdles* add a tablespoon of cold milk and use your mixer or a blender to beat the cream until smooth.

Top this vanilla ice cream with a chocolate sauce or fresh fruit to make a wonderful dessert.

Store tightly covered in your freezer for up to two weeks.

CHOCOLATE ICE CREAM

Follow the methods used in making vanilla ice cream to make chocolate ice cream.

INGREDIENTS

3 1/4 cups of milk

1 cup granulated sugar

6 egg yolks

6 tablespoons of cocoa powder in a large bowl

METHOD

- Cook the cream as described in the Vanilla ice cream methods. After the cream is cooked, but before it is cool *add the cream* a tablespoon at a time to the bowl containing the cocoa. Either use a whisk to stir it in, or a mixer to stir it in completely. Cool the cream over ice cubes the same way as described in making vanilla ice cream.

- After cooling completely, pour the cream into your freezer and freeze according to its directions.

Serve chocolate ice cream with a chocolate sauce sprinkled with nuts or with a scoop of vanilla ice cream. This recipe makes great molded desserts and filling for cream puffs.

MOLDING ICE CREAM

- Place the mold in the freezer and allow to become very cold.

- Add the ice cream to the mold as soon as in comes from the ice cream freezer. Freeze until the ice cream has hardened.
- Place the molded ice cream in the refrigerator for about 30 minutes before serving. Remove the mold from the ice cream by dipping it in hot water for about 5 seconds. Quickly turn upside down and tap gently until the ice cream releases. If the ice cream will not release—repeat the hot water dip and use a spatula to pry it out. Place the un-molded ice cream back into the freezer for a few minutes to refreeze the melted outside edge.

SOLUTIONS

QUESTION: *Why does my fudge get hard and gritty after a day or two?*

ANSWER: If you are using cocoa in the recipe you should add a tablespoon of corn syrup, honey or salad oil. This should help keep the fudge soft for a longer time.

When you over cook the fudge it will also become too hard. Use a candy thermometer whenever you make candy and watch it carefully.

Cover the fudge tightly *after it cools* so that it won't dry out.

Over beating will cause fudge to become too hard. Follow the recipe's instructions, but if the fudge thickens quickly stop beating and pour it up. The temperature of the room and nuts (if you add them) will sometimes cause fudge to thicken quickly.

QUESTION: *Is there anything I can do to make my scratch chocolate cake more moist?*

ANSWER: You may add an extra egg yolk, a tablespoon of salad oil or use melted semi-sweet chocolate instead of cocoa. If you don't want the extra fats—replace 1/3 of the water with apple sauce.

Drizzle a warm simple syrup sauce over warm chocolate cake layers before applying the frosting. Let the layers finish cooling and then ice as usual.

QUESTION: *What can I do to make a box of brownie mix taste special?*

ANSWER: Add a tablespoon of honey, a tablespoon of melted butter and a third of a cup of pecans or walnuts to the dry mix. Follow the mixing and baking directions on the package.

QUESTION: *Why are my chocolate cupcakes always very dry? My chocolate cake is perfect.*

ANSWER: Bake chocolate cupcakes at a ten degree higher temperature than cake. The cupcakes should be done in about twelve minutes. Over-baking is the common cause of dry cupcakes, so watch them carefully.

QUESTION: *My chocolate cake is full of holes (tunnels) after it is baked. What am I doing wrong?*

ANSWER: When the cake batter is too thick it will sometimes cause tunnels as air bubbles come to the surface during baking. If you are following the recipe carefully and the cake layers are tunneled you may need to add a little extra liquid to the mix. This problem happens when ingredients are used that were not of the same brand name as was used in the original recipe. Using all purpose flour instead of cake flour would be an example.

QUESTION: *Why does my chocolate cake peak and split in the middle during baking?*

ANSWER: Your oven is probably too hot. Try lowering the temperature about ten degrees. You may be placing the cake pans too close to the back or sides of the oven when it is best to place them in the center and on the center shelf.

QUESTION: *Why is my chocolate butter cream frosting too pale and almost flavorless?*

ANSWER: Over-mixing the frosting and not enough cocoa or chocolate will cause the frosting to be light in color. Add more cocoa for flavor. Melt semi-sweet chocolate and thin with whipping cream then add to the frosting for flavor. Add a little orange extract for a special taste.

QUESTION: *My chocolate pie filling is too runny? What can I do to thicken it up and not change the taste.*

ANSWER: Cook the filling until it coats a metal spoon. Under-cooking will cause the filling to be very soft. Remove some of the liquid from the recipe and the filling will cook thicker. Make sure you are using the same brand name ingredients the recipe calls for. If the recipe calls for evaporated milk—don't use whole milk. If you substitute dry milk for fresh make sure the liquids are kept in balance by reconstituting the milk first and not adding just the milk powder to the recipe.

APPENDIX

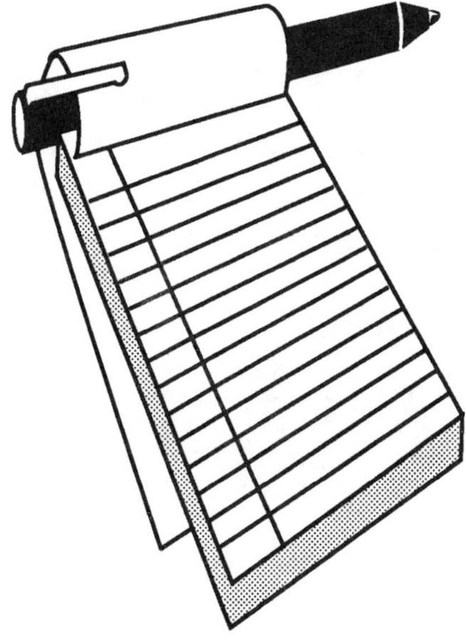

Contents

APPENDIX

CHOCOLATE FACTS

You can substitute cocoa for chocolate in your favorite recipe.

Substitute 3 level tablespoons cocoa plus 1 tablespoon shortening (melted or solid) for 1 block (1 ounce) of unsweetened baking chocolate.

Substitute 6 tablespoons cocoa, plus 7 tablespoons granulated sugar, plus 1/4 cup shortening (melted or solid) for one 6 ounce package of semi-sweet chocolate chips or 6 blocks of semi-sweet chocolate.

Substitute 3 tablespoons cocoa, plus 4 1/2 tablespoons sugar, plus 2 2/3 tablespoons shortening (melted or solid) for one 4 ounce bar of sweet baking chocolate.

Note → Chocolate will store for about one year in a cool, dry place at between 65 and 70 degrees. When chocolate is stored for a length of time at higher temperatures, bloom will occur and a gray or white haze will form on top of the chocolate. This haze will not affect the quality or the taste of the chocolate. In high humidity storage, chocolate will mold quickly.

Melt chocolate in a double boiler over low heat. Never let water, even a few drops, get into melting chocolate. The chocolate will become grainy and stiff. When this happens, stir in 1 teaspoon of solid vegetable shortening (not butter) for each 2 ounces of chocolate.

Melt chocolate in your microwave oven. Use a micro-proof bowl and use full power. To melt unsweetened baking chocolate and semi-sweet chocolate.

1 block - set time 1 to 1 1/2 minutes. 2 blocks - set time 1 1/2 to 2 minutes. 3 blocks - set time 2 to 2 1/2 minutes 4 blocks - set time 2 1/2 to 3 minutes. Let the chocolate sit for a little while, then stir to make it fluid.

Melt chocolate chips (6 ounces) by using full power for about 1 1/2 minutes. Stir, then allow to stand for several minutes and stir again.

Chocolate and cocoa will absorb odors and chocolate will become rancid because of poor storage. Cocoa will become lumpy when allowed to absorb moisture.

Sift cocoa because the lumps will not dissolve in your cakes and frosting.

Please read the chapter about chocolate for more information about this wonderful ingredient.

DEFINITION OF INGREDIENTS

WHEAT FLOUR:

Short—Fancy Patent Flour: These are the best grades of flours. They are milled from the best portions of the endosperm. They have less protein than some of the other grades of flour, but it is of the highest quality.

Bakers—Long Patent Flour: These are good flours for regular bread, but the protein is not as high as in the Short Patent Flour.

Bromated Flours: These flours are high in gluten content and high in protein. Good for French Bread and other breads when a tough, chewy, texture is desired.

Whole Wheat Flours: The entire wheat grain is ground to make 100% whole wheat or Graham Flour.

Cake Flour: These flours are milled from soft winter wheat. They are always ground finer than bread flours.

Pastry Flour: These flours are milled from soft winter wheat which contain a larger amount of protein, or from hard winter wheat which has a low protein content.

SALT: Salt (sodium chloride). Salt is used to enhance the flavor of other ingredients in baked products. It also has a strengthening effect on the gluten in flours.

YEAST: Yeast is a microscopic one-cell plant.

The enzymes contained in the yeast plant produce chemical changes in a product, but does not enter into them.

The enzymes are: (a) Sucrose which converts sucrose (sugar) into dextrose and levulose, forms used by yeast as food. (b) Maltase, which converts (maltose) into dextrose. (c) Zymase, which changes dextrose and levulose into carbon dioxide gas and alcohol producing fermentation. (d) Proteolytic enzymes, which acts on the complex proteins converting them into simpler, more soluble forms, aiding in gluten conditioning.

SUGAR: These are compounds which contain carbon, hydrogen, and oxygen, with hydrogen and oxygen in the proportion found in water. These are known as carbohydrates. All sugars are in this class of compounds.

The order of sweetness (to taste) is: **Cane sugar, Beet sugar, Corn sugar, Lactose.**

Sugar is used in baked products to: Tenderize the protein of the flour. Adds sweetness. Causes a good crust color. Retains moisture and prolongs the freshness of a product.

Cane and **Beet** sugar are 99.5% pure sucrose.

Brown Sugars are made by crystallizing the final syrup, after white sugar has been refined. They contain 3 to 4% more moisture than white sugar.

Invert Sugar is an equal blend of dextrose and Levulose.

SHORTENING: Butter is milk fat, which contains a small percentage of salt, milk solids and moisture.

Hydrogenated Shortening is made usually of a vegetable oil which is processed by a hydrogenation agent. This shortening can be made harder or softer by the amount of processing used. In this manner, winter and summer shortenings are made.

Emulsified type shortenings are made by adding mono and diglycerides to hydrogenated shortening. This shortening made to be used in cakes and icings where high emulsifying properties are necessary.

Donut (Frying) Shortening is hydrogenated shortening which is processed to a greater hardness to aid in stability. It has a good keeping quality.

MILK: Milk is used to: Improve crust color (50% lactose), Increase yield, increased flavor, increased fermentation tolerance, improves grain and texture. Sweetened Condensed milk contains about 42% cane or beet sugar.

BAKING TEMPERATURE

Differences in temperature are controlled by the size of the baked item, its raw temperature, the richness of its ingredients and the desired crust color and texture. Pan size and type also are factors that must be considered when making decisions on baking temperature. Cookies in particular require practice to find the exact baking temperature that suits your baking environment.

Sometimes it's necessary to bake on *double pans* in order to keep the bottom crust from burning. Sometimes things must be covered during the bake in order to get the perfect top color. There are no set rules. Don't be tied by the boundaries written in the recipe. The recipe is a guide and your baking environment will be different than any other. Experiment—and become a great baker.

OVEN TEMPERATURES

Very slow 250—275 degrees Fahrenheit
Slow 300—325 degrees Fahrenheit
Moderate 350—375 degrees Fahrenheit
Moderately hot 400 degrees Fahrenheit
Hot 425 degrees Fahrenheit
Very hot 450—475 degrees Fahrenheit
Broil 500—525 degrees Fahrenheit
When using a glass or thin aluminum baking pan, lower the temperature about 25 degrees F.

BREAD, QUICK BREAD, SWEETBREAD

White bread loaves	350-375
White bread rolls	365-385
Egg breads (Challah)	350-365
French and Italian loaves	385-410
French and Italian rolls	400-425
Raisin bread loaves	350-365
Cinnamon bread loaves	350-365
Dinner rolls	365-385
Biscuits	365-400
Popovers	400-425
Quick breads	350-385
Muffins	375-390
Coffee Cakes (large)	350-365
Cinnamon rolls	350-375
Sweet rolls (danish)	360-385
Puff Pastry Turnovers	385-410
Cream Puff Shells	425 then down to 365
Eclair Shells	425 then down to 365
Pizza Crust (not topped)	400-450
Corn bread (muffins)	400-425

CAKES, CUPCAKES

Cheese Cakes	365-375
Chiffon Cake	350-365
Angel Food Cake	350-365
White layer Cake	350-365
Chocolate layer Cake	350-375
Yellow layer Cake	350-375
Jelly rolls	375-385
Cupcake	355-375
Pound Cake (large)	350-365
Pound Cake (small)	365-375
Fruit Cake (large)	290-310
Fruit Cake (small)	300-315

PIES, TARTS

Fruit Pies 365-385
Fruit Tarts 375-385
Custard Pie 350-365
Pumpkin Pie 350-390
Pie Shells 365-385
Pecan Pie 300-325

COOKIES

Sugar Cookies (small) 355-365
Sugar Cookies (cutout) 350-365
Kisses (meringue) 200
Oatmeal Cookies 350-365
Peanut Butter Cookies 350-365
Bar Type Cookies 355-365
Coconut Macaroons 350-375
Sand Tart Cookies 350-365
Chocolate Chip Cookies 355-375
Icebox Cookies 355-375
Vanilla Wafer Cookies 365-375
Ginger Snaps 365-380

GLOSSARY

ABSORB: To take in by chemical or molecular action.

ALBUMEN: The white of an egg.

ALMOND PASTE: A mixture of 2/3 sugar and 1/3 ground almonds.

BAIN MARIE: A double boiler.

BAG OUT: To press dough, batter, or frosting from a conical shaped cloth, or paper bag.

BAKE: To cook in an oven usually with dry heat.

BAKING POWDER: A mixture of chemicals which, when heated, generates CO_2 gas. The gas aerates baked products causing them to rise.

BAKING SODA: Bicarbonate of soda.

BATCH: The entire contents of a recipe.

BEAT: To aerate a mixture by beating together with a spoon, fork, whisk, or electric mixer.

BLANCH: To parboil for a minute or two or pour boiling water over food, or to dip briefly in boiling water.

BLEND: To fold or mix two or more ingredients together to obtain equal distribution.

BOILING POINT: Water boils at 212 degrees Fahrenheit.

BREAD: To roll or cover food with crumbs. Usually the food is first dipped in milk or whipped egg.

CARAMEL: Sugar heated above its melting point so that it takes on an amber color.

CARAMELIZE: Describes the color change in sugar.

CHOCOLATE: A product of the roasted Cacao bean. Cacao trees grow only 20 degrees north and south of the Equator and mainly in West Africa and Latin America. Chocolate liquor, Cocoa Butter, Cocoa Powder, Dutch-Process

Cocoa Powder, Bitter Chocolate, Semi-Sweet Chocolate, Sweet Chocolate and Milk Chocolate are all products of the Cocoa bean.

CHOP: To cut into small pieces.

CINNAMON: Cinnamon is ground from the inter-bark of a type of laurel tree. Cinnamon varies in strength and loses its flavor with age.

CLARIFY: The removal of extraneous material from a liquid. Usually the removal of water from the oil in butter.

CLOVE: A clove is the dried bud of a species of myrtle grown in Zanzibar and the East Indies.

COOL: To let food stand at room temperature until it is no longer warm to the touch.

COUVERTURE: A chocolate which has been correctly tempered before use to make a fine gloss on finish products.

CREAM: To beat fat and sugar or flour together until the mixture is light and fluffy.

CRYSTALIZATION: The forming of sugar into crystals.

DEVELOP: To mix a bread type dough to increase its elasticity by the development of the flour's gluten.

DISSOLVING: The act of liquefying a solid.

DOCKING: To punch holes in a yeast dough in order to insure a texture without large holes.

DUST: To sprinkle flour on a working surface to keep dough from sticking.

EGG: A fresh egg is made up of three parts; the shell is 12%, the white is 58%, the yolk is 30%. An egg white has .25% fat content. An egg yolk has 31 to 32% fat content. An egg white has 12% protein. An egg yolk has 16% protein.

EGG WASH: To brush on a mixture of fresh egg and water to make breads and rolls have a shine to their crusts.

EMULSIFIED SHORTENING: Is shortening to which an emulsifer has been add. This shortening will hold moisture in baked items.

ENROBE: To coat with icing, chocolate. Cakes, cookies

and pastries are enrobed with a coating.

FLOUR: The wheat grain has three main parts. The bran coating is about 13%. The Embryo or germ is about 2%. The Endosperm is about 85%. The Endosperm consists of protein, starch, fat, water, sugar and mineral matter. White flour is milled from the endosperm.

FRY: To cook in fat.

FOLD: To mix together by a gentle over and under method.

GINGER: Ginger is made from the root of a herb grown in China, India, Australia and South Africa.

GLAZE: To give a glossy surface to baked products.

GLUCOSE: A very thick corn syrup. In most cases a light corn syrup can be substituted in the recipe.

GLUTEN: The insoluble wheat protein left after hydration. Gluten is the elastic substance that assists in trapping Co^2 gas in a bread dough. The strength of the flour's gluten determines the toughness of the dough or batter. Bread dough requires a high gluten strength, while cake batter requires low gluten strength.

HONEY: Honey is produced by bees from the nectar of flowers. The flavor of honey depends on the kind of flowers the bee finds. Clover honey is what we consider the best.

GREASING: The process of applying a thin coating of shortening inside a cake or pie pan to prevent sticking.

HYGROSCOPIC: The power to attract moisture.

KNEAD: To work ingredients into a mass of bread dough by mixing, usually by hand.

LEAVENING: A substance which, when exposed to liquid or heat, produces a gas causing aeration before or during baking.

MILK: Milk is variable in composition. An average composition is; Fat 3.75%, Milk protein 3.46%, Mineral matter .75%, Lactose 4.70% and Water 87.34%. Milk has a fairly high sugar content which helps browning. The fat with the sugar enriches and tenderizes baked goods.

MIXING: The blending of ingredients into a mass.

MOULD: To shape dough into loaves or rolls by hand or machine.

NUTMEG: Nutmeg is ground from the nut of the Nutmeg tree. Nutmeg comes from the East and West Indies. Mace comes from the same fruit.

OIL: Pure vegetable oil, Olive oil and Palm oil are used in baking. Vegetable oil is used in Sponge type cakes and to make solid shortening and margarine. Olive oil is used in bread. Palm oil is used to make solid vegetable shortening.

OVER-MIX: To mix longer than the recipe can tolerate.

PROOF: To let yeast type doughs rise.

ROUNDING: To shape bread dough into a tight ball. Rounding puts bread dough in a proofing stage, before the final shape is made.

SCALD: To heat milk to just below the boiling point.

SCALING: Weighing ingredients on a scale.

SET or SET-UP: Terms use to descripe something that changes consistency usually upon cooling, such as gelatin.

SIFTING: To shake dry ingredients through a fine mesh screen called a sieve.

SALT: Salt is sodium chloride. Salt is composed of 40% sodium and 60% chloride. It adds a flavor of its own to baked products and also slightly enhances the flavors of other ingredients. Salt has a retarding effect on yeast and a toughening effect on gluten.

SHORTENING: Shortening is the fat used in baking. Butter, vegetable shortening, margarine and lard are shortenings.

STIRRING: Using a spoon or whisk to mix ingredients or to cause dissolving.

SUGAR: Granulated sugar, Powdered sugar and Brown sugar are the most common sugars used in baking. Refined sugar comes from sugar cane or sugar beets. Cane and beet sugar is call sucrose and are equally sweet.

SYRUP: Light and dark corn syrup, glucose, molasses and honey are the most common syrups used in baking.

TEMPERATURE: The degree of cold or heat.

TEMPERING: To regulate a liquid temperature to a desired requirement.

TEXTURE: The inside size of grain or smoothness of a baked item.

UNDER-MIX: To mix a recipe too little.

WASH: To brush a liquid over the top of any baked item—before, during, or after baking.

WET PEAK: A stage where the meringue peak folds over.

WHIP: A whisk.

WHIPPING: Using a hand whisk or a mixer attachment to beat ingredients. Usually eggs or heavy cream.

YEAST: Yeast is a living micro-organism of the fungi family of plants. Yeast is the primary rising ingredient in bread. Yeast should be stored at 40 degrees F and has a thermal death point of 140 degrees F. Yeast can be purchased as fresh compressed, dried, or instant dried.

ZEST: The outer rind of oranges and lemons. The zest contains the oil of the fruit.

FREEZING TABLES 

Water freezes at 32 degrees Fahrenheit: 0 degrees Centigrade

The most important thing to remember about freezing is making sure that the freezer is at 0 degrees or below. Keep a freezer thermometer in the freezer and check it periodically. Almost all baked or raw items will freeze well. Make the most of your baking time by making some for now and freezing some for later.

The freezing tables give maximum freezing times. When the freezer fails because of a power failure—do not open it. Baked items will stay frozen for about two days. When the freezer will be off longer than that—refrigerate what you can and bake off the rest.

Use only containers and wraps suitable for freezing. They must be moisture and vapor proof. Heavy foil or heavy plastic bags are recommended. Make sure that everything is sealed airtight. Always label all packages with the contents and the date. Adding the (use-by) date is also a good idea. Package in amounts that will be used at one time.

FREEZING BREADS

LOAVES

Cool quickly, wrap and freeze. Do not cool in a draft. Thaw at room temperature for 2 to 3 hours in wrap. (Will freeze for 2 months.)

ROLLS

Cool quickly, wrap and freeze in foil. Thaw at room temperature in the foil or in a 275 degree oven for about 15 minutes. Use at once. (Will freeze for 2 months.)

CINNAMON AND SWEET ROLLS

Cool quickly, wrap and freeze in foil. Thaw at room temperature in the foil or heat in a 275 degree oven for about 15 minutes. Apply icing while the rolls are warm and serve at once. (Will freeze for 2 months.)

BISCUITS

Cool quickly, wrap in foil and freeze. Thaw in a 325 degree oven for about 15 minutes. Remove the foil before heating. (Will freeze for 2 months.)

DOUGHNUTS

Cool quickly, wrap in foil and freeze. Heat uncovered in a 275 degree oven for about 15 minutes and glaze while hot. Serve at once. (Will freeze 1 month.)

MUFFINS

Cool quickly, wrap in foil and freeze. Thaw in the foil at room temperature or heat in a 275 degree oven for about 20 minutes. (Will freeze for 2 months.)

CAKES IN GENERAL

Remove from the pan and cool quickly. Wrap single layers in foil or place in a heavy plastic freezer bag. When you want to freeze a frosted cake—freeze the cake first with no wrapping, then wrap it. Single uniced layers will freeze better.

Thaw—wrapped at room temperature for about 2 hours then frost as desired. Do not freeze boiled type frostings or meringue type frostings.

Single layers will freeze for 3 months. Airtight seal is a must.

Frosting made with powdered sugar and shortening or butter will freeze for about 2 months. We recommend that you use fresh frosting.

COOKIES

RAW DOUGH: Wrap dough in foil and freeze. Thaw in the wrap, then bake. (Will freeze 1 year.)

Baked: Cool quickly. Wrap in foil or put in an airtight container and freeze. Thaw in the package or heat in the oven or microwave until warm. (Will freeze 1 year.)

PIE CRUSTS

RAW: Make into crusts. Wrap and freeze. Will freeze 2 months. Bake frozen crusts the same as fresh.

BAKED: Make into crusts. Bake. Cool quickly, wrap and freeze. Thaw at room temperature or use at once. (Will freeze for 2 months.)

PIES

RAW: Don't slit the top crust. Wrap and freeze. Do not thaw before baking. Remove the wrap, slit the top and bake as usual (425 degrees for 20 minutes then at 365 degrees until done.) Some berry or cherry pies should be baked at 385 degrees throughout the bake time. (Will freeze for 2 months.)

BAKED: Cool quickly wrap and freeze. (Will freeze for 2 months.) Thaw in the wrap at room temperature or heat unwrapped for 20 minutes at about 275 degrees.

WEIGHTS—METRIC EQUIVALENT

1 ounce = 28.35 grams
1 gallon = 3.79 liter
1 liter = 2.11 pints
1 liter = 1.06 quarts
1 liter = 0.26 gallons
1 quart = 0.95 liter
1 pound = 0.45 kilograms
1 gram = .04 ounces
1 kilogram = 2.20 pounds
1 pint = 0.47 liter

BASIC MEASUREMENTS—WEIGHTS

3 tsp = 1 tbsp
4 tbsp = 1/4 cup
8 tbsp = 1/2 cup
5 tbsp + 1 tsp = 1/3 cup
8 oz (water) = 1 cup
1 cup = 1/2 pint
2 cups = 1 pint
4 cups = 1 quart
1 pint = 16 oz (water)
2 pints = 1 quart = 32 oz
4 quarts = 1 gallon

INGREDIENT WEIGHTS—MEASURES

Almonds (whole) 1 lb .... 4 1/2 cups
Apples (chopped) about 3 large .... 3 cups
Baking soda 1 oz. .... 2 tbsp
Baking powder 1 oz .... 2 1/2 tbsp
Butter (Margarine) 1 lb .... 2 cups
Bananas (sliced) 1 lb .... 2 1/2 cups
Bananas (3 mashed) .... 1 cup
Berries (cleaned) 1 qt .... 3 1/2 cups

Cardamon (ground) 1 oz .... 5 tbsp
Chocolate (grated) 1 oz .... 4 tbsp
Chocolate (morsels) 6 oz .... 1 cup
Cinnamon (ground) 1 oz .... 4 1/2 tbsp
Cocoa 1 lb .... 4 1/4 cups
Coconut (shredded) 1 lb .... 5 1/2 cups
Corn meal 1 lb .... 3 cups
Corn syrup 1 lb .... 1 1/2 cups
Cornstarch 1 oz .... 2 1/4 tbsps
Cranberries (whole) 1 lb .... 4 cups
Cream (fresh) 1 pt .... 2 cups
Cream of Tartar 1 oz .... 3 tbsps
Eggs (Whole) 4 or 5 .... 1 cup
Eggs (Whole) 2 lb .... 1 qt
Eggs (Whole) 1 lb 10
Egg whites 8-10 .... 1 cup
Egg whites 1 lb 16
Egg yolks 12-14 .... 1 cup
Egg yolks 1 lb 24
Flour (bread or all-purpose) 1 lb .... 3 1/2 cups
Flour (cake) 1 lb .... 4 1/2 cups
Flour (whole wheat) 1 lb .... 3 1/2 cups
Gelatin 1 oz .... 4 tbsps
Gelatin (thickens liquid) .... 1 tbsp to 2 cups.
Honey 12 oz .... 1 cup
Lemon juice 8 oz .... 1 cup
Milk (liquid) 8 oz .... 1 cup
Milk (powdered) 4 oz .... 1 cup
Molasses 12 oz .... 1 cup
Nut-meats (chopped) 1 lb .... 3 cups
Oil (vegetable) 8 oz .... 1 cup
Peanut Butter 1 lb .... 2 cups
Raisins 1 lb .... 3 cups
Rice 1 lb .... 2 1/4 cups
Rolled Oats 1 lb .... 5 cups
Shortening 1 lb .... 2 1/2 cups
Sugar (brown) 1 lb .... 2 cups
Sugar (granulated) 1 lb .... 2 cups
Sugar (powdered) 1 lb .... 3 1/2 cups
Vanilla 1 oz .... 2 tbsps

SUBSTITUTIONS

Baking Power = 2 tablespoons cream of tartar, 1 tablespoon baking soda, 1 tablespoon corn starch. (sift together) *Single action Baking Powder.*

1 cup self rising flour=1 cup flour plus 1 1/2 tsp baking powder and 1/2 tsp salt

l cup cake flour .... 1 cup minus 2 tsp all purpose flour

1 tablespoon cornstarch .... 2 tablespoons all-purpose flour

1 cup whole milk .... 1/2 cup evaporated milk + 1/2 cup water

1 cup sour or buttermilk=1 tablespoon lemon juice or vinegar plus sweet milk to make 1 cup. (let stand 5 minutes)

1 oz unsweetened chocolate = 3 tbsps cocoa powder + 1 tbsp butter or margarine.

1 cup honey, corn syrup .... 3/4 cup sugar + 1/4 cup water

1 teaspoon pumpkin pie spice .... 1/2 teaspoon cinnamon, 1/4 tsp. ginger, 1/8 tsp. allspice, 1/8 tsp. cardamon

1 cup cream, sour, heavy, ... 1/3 cup butter + 2/3 cup milk

1 package dry yeast .... 1 cake compressed yeast

CAKE SERVING

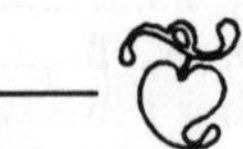

8-inch round will serve 10 to 12

9-inch round will serve 12 to 14

13 x 9 x 2-inch will serve 12 to 14

10-inch angel food will serve 12 to 14

SUBSTITUTION OF CAKE PANS

Use:	or	Use:
1—8 x 8 x 2 square		1—9-inch round
2—8 x 8 x 2 square		2—9-inch round
or		1—19 x 19 x 2-inch
2—8-inch round		2 thin 8 x 8 x 2-inch
or		18 to 24 cupcakes
3—8-inch round		2—9 x 9 x 2-inch
2—9-inch round		2—8 x 8 x 2-inch
or		3 thin 8-inch round
or		1—15 x 10 x 1-inch
or		30 cupcakes
1—9 x 9 x 1-inch		2 thin 8-inch round
1—19 x 9 x 2-inch		3—8-inch round
1—9 x 5 x 3-inch loaf		1—9 x 9 x 2-inch
or		24 to 30 cupcakes
1—9 x 3 1/2-inch tube		2—9-inch round
or		20 cupcakes
1—10 x 4-inch tube		2—9 x 5 x 3-inch loaf
or		1—13 x 9 x 2-inch

Your Notes

Your grocer's shelves are stacked high with wonderful pre-mixed boxes of different items for you to bake. Try something new and surprise everyone.

Index

C

D

E

F

L

M

N

O

P

THANKS

to ALL the wonderful people who made this book possible.

- ☺ Edna, Marcie and Charles for their continued faith
- ☺ Sue-Ki and Natasha for their enduring patience
- ☺ The professional bakers for their tips
- ☺ Our families & friends for their support
- ☺ McNaughton & Gunn, Inc. for the printing

A Special Note to You

Every day untold thousands of people bake goodies in their home kitchens. Almost all of them want what they bake to look appetizing and taste good. We have done our best to make this book answer the questions and solve the baking problems that these people have.

Baking Solutions was built upon the foundation of two worlds of baking. Kenneth Power built his foundation in professional baking kitchens. Lyndal Power built her foundation in a home kitchen. The combining of two lifetimes in baking, along with considerable advice from others, caused *Baking Solutions* to be created.

As you use *Baking Solutions* we know that you will improve your baking skills. As your skills improve you'll bake more often because you will enjoy it more. If you apply the idea of having love for the right method and the desire to do things with a reason—in proven ways, the other things you do will also improve.

We had a lot of fun putting together *Baking Solutions* and hope you'll enjoy it. We know you'll learn something from reading it.

Also available from YCART Publishing.

POWER BAKING, A Contemporary American Baking Manual by Kenneth Power is written for professional food service workers who bake.

Kenneth Power uses his 30 plus years as a professional baker to teach others the secrets of making perfect baked products.

POWER BAKING includes hundreds of tried recipes and assembly methods. It's tips, suggestions, new ideas, forms, conversion tables and extra large print makes it a baking tool every professional and serious home baker can use. It is an excellent reference source.

ISBN: 1-880650-14-2

Softcover, 8.5 x 11 inches, 512 pages $39.95

NEED ADDITIONAL COPIES?

Use these handy order blanks

✂

POWER BAKING ❖ YCART PUBLISHING ❖ P.O. BOX 74980 ❖ OKLAHOMA CITY ❖ OK ❖ 73147-0980

Please send me ______ copy/copies of ***POWER BAKING*** at **$ 41.95** each—including shipping.

My check or money order is enclosed for a total amount of — $__________

Oklahoma residents please add appropriate sales tax.

NAME:____

ADDRESS:______________________________________

CITY:__________________STATE:_______ ZIP:________

✂

BAKING SOLUTIONS ❖ YCART PUBLISHING ❖ P.O. BOX 74980 ❖ OKLAHOMA CITY ❖ OK ❖ 73147-0980

Please send me ______ copy/copies of BAKING SOLUTIONS at $ **14.95** each—including shipping.

My check or money order is enclosed for a total amount of — $__________

Oklahoma residents please add appropriate sales tax.

NAME:____

ADDRESS:______________________________________

CITY:__________________STATE:______ZIP:________

Good
Baking
Award
As a user of this
book. You are
hereby awarded
this certificate of
good baking.